as College history at a glance.

1931

e

cation at Marywood motherhouse

1931–1940

Catholic Junior College

Expanded curriculum co-educational Catholic junior college

1940–present

Aquinas College

Four-year liberal arts college

Aquinas College

THE FIRST 125 YEARS

PRAYER • STUDY • SERVICE • COMMUNITY
AQUINAS • COLLEGE
NON NISI TE, DOMINE
GRAND RAPIDS • MICHIGAN
125 YEARS

Aquinas College

THE FIRST 125 YEARS

THE DONNING COMPANY PUBLISHERS

The Donning Company Publishers
184 Business Park Drive, Suite 206
Virginia Beach, VA 23462

Steve Mull, General Manager
Barbara B. Buchanan, Office Manager
Richard A. Horwege, Senior Editor
Amanda Dawn Guilmain, Graphic Designer
Priscilla Odango, Imaging Artist
Steve Hartman, Project Research Coordinator
Tonya Hannink, Marketing Specialist
Pamela Engelhard, Marketing Advisor

G. Bradley Martin, Project Director

Library of Congress Cataloging-in-Publication Data

Eberle, Gary.
Aquinas College : the first 125 years / by Gary Eberle.
p. cm.
Includes index.
ISBN 978-1-57864-695-1 (hard cover : alk. paper)
1. Aquinas College (Grand Rapids, Mich.)—History. 2. Aquinas College (Grand Rapids, Mich.)—History—Pictorial works. I. Title.
LD177.E34 2011
378.774'56—dc23

2011032599

Printed in the USA at Walsworth Publishing Company

Contents

Introduction

PRAYER, STUDY, SERVICE, AND COMMUNITY

Prayer, study, service, and community: These four Dominican charisms have defined the development of Aquinas College from its beginning. A charism is a gift of the Spirit, given for the benefit of others. Through the past 125 years, the college has kept true to its founding gifts. As it went through periodic growing pains and financial crises, as it weathered two world wars, the Great Depression, and the social upheavals of the late twentieth century, the college's administration, faculty, staff, students, and alumni recognized that what made Aquinas uniquely itself was its adherence to the Catholic Dominican tradition which rests on the four charisms that we celebrate in this commemorative history book.

Study, prayer, service, and community are the themes that run through this short history. The gift of study is obvious. Aquinas is, after all, a college, founded in the liberal arts tradition that began in the European Middle Ages. The charism of prayer is equally obvious. Founded by a religious order of women and staffed primarily by religious sisters and priests during its first sixty or more years, Aquinas College has always recognized that the life of the mind and the life of the spirit are interfused. That is the legacy of the Catholic intellectual tradition that reaches all the way back to St. Dominic and before. As the many photos in this book will show, the sacramental life of the Catholic Church was, and is, the source of the college's constant self-renewal.

The college's emphasis on service is also one of its hallmarks. Throughout its history, Aquinas College and its predecessor schools were not just institutions of book learning and job preparation. From the start, the college called on itself to serve the world, from the original teaching sisters of the order who staffed parish schools in northern and western Michigan in the 1800s, to the men and women who enlisted in the armed services, to the various groups of students and staff who took service trips to Appalachia with Father Bukowski in the 1950s, or those in the college who helped found the Eastown Community Association in the 1960s. Today, under a full-time director of Service Learning, students, faculty, and staff still serve the west Michigan community and such far-off fields as Haiti, Mexico, and the Dominican Republic.

All of this has fostered the growth of a strong community, which often refers to itself as the Aquinas "family," and that sense of an enduring community is one of Aquinas's greatest gifts. It brings alumni back on Homecoming Weekend, and it sustains us in times

of personal and institutional crisis. Community is what we celebrate throughout the year at our reunions and events, and in the regular rituals of the academic year.

Like every vital institution, Aquinas College, founded as Novitiate Normal School in 1886, goes on refounding itself every day. It continues to grow and change as it responds to the changing world, and we believe that far into the future the college will continue to hold true to its founding values and maintain a firm belief in the necessary interaction of study, prayer, service, and community.

Writing a book is a collaborative process, so I would like to thank the following people. First, Sisters Jean Milhaupt, Rose Marie Martin, and Michael Ellen Carling, O.P., for help in retrieving material from the Marywood and Aquinas College archives. Sister Jean especially was a fount of knowledge and became, for me, the living history of the college. Sister Michael Ellen was most helpful in finding original prints of old photos, and Sister Mona Schwind's history of the Dominican sisters of Grand Rapids, *Period Pieces*, was an important source for the earliest days through the early 1960s. For help in transcribing the oral history texts of *Speaking Historically*, I thank Jill Straub, Dr. Ian Borton, and Tony Nolan. The five-disk oral history of the college, released in 1997, was the result of hundreds of hours of taped interviews conducted by the Aquinas College Historical Commission. Thanks are also due to the current Aquinas College Historical Commission members who read the first drafts of this book and gave invaluable editorial advice on content and pictures, and to the Aquinas College Media Department for technical and design support. And special thanks are also due to the mostly uncredited photographers from the early years whose work helps illustrate this book and provides us with an invaluable window into our past.

Chapter 1

Novitiate Normal School
TO CATHOLIC JUNIOR COLLEGE 1886–1931

A Vision and a Mission

In May 1877, Mother Augustine Neuhierl, prioress of a group of Dominican sisters originally from Regensburg, Germany, lay on her deathbed in Holy Rosary convent on East Second Street in New York City. She had been in the United States since 1853, when she and three other sisters arrived in the New World to work with the growing Catholic immigrant population. By 1877, her New York community numbered ninety-five sisters. As she neared her end, Mother Augustine told the sisters gathered by her deathbed she had just seen a vision. She reported, "somewhere in the West, I see a vast field of labor—an inland island—and as a field is dotted white with daisies, so this land will be dotted white with the habit of St. Dominic."[1]

The sisters did not know what to make of this, but several months after Mother Augustine's death, a call came for sisters to teach in the then pioneer town of Traverse City, Michigan. Father George Ziegler, pastor of newly formed St. Francis Parish, had written to a priest friend in New Jersey to ask him to help find teachers for the school he wanted to start for the children of his church. He did not have much to offer in the way of inducements, and several communities of sisters had already rejected his request for help.[2] Finally, Ziegler's call reached Mother Hyacinth Scheininger, Mother Augustine's successor, who summoned twenty-nine-year-old Sister Aquinata Fiegler and sent her and five other young nuns on the nine-hundred-mile journey to the rugged lumber and port town of Traverse City. Mother Aquinata, in her memoir, believed that Mother Hyacinth's quick reply to Ziegler's request was because she connected this call for service with Mother Augustine's vision. Though Michigan, being composed of two peninsulas, was not *quite* an island, it was a new field of activity in the west for the Dominicans.

The five young sisters—Aquinata, Boniface, Angela, Camilla, Borromeo, and Martha—left New York on

Mother Aquinata Fiegler led a group of five young nuns to Traverse City in 1877 and founded what would become Novitiate Normal School in 1886. The Normal School eventually evolved into Aquinas College.

Sisters who were trained at Novitiate Normal School taught at Catholic elementary schools across Michigan. Here, Sisters Berchmans and Reginald sit in a horse and buggy outside St. Mary's Academy in Carson City. Two unidentified sisters stand behind the fence.

spent a busy weekend readying their home and their classroom for the beginning of school the following Monday. Bright and early, the first six pupils arrived at the new St. Francis School and began their education. The early years in Traverse City were hard, marked by financial difficulties for the fledgling parish and school. Often, the poor parishioners paid their tuition in kind, offering food in exchange for the sisters' work. The sisters also supplemented their income by giving language lessons and taking in needlework at night. As was true in most Catholic schools of the time, the sisters were not paid much for this work. Teaching was their ministry, and Catholic schools depended on the contributed services of the teaching nuns.

October 15, 1877, and arrived in Traverse City on October 25.[3] The journey by rail, horse and buggy, steamship, and wagon was described by Mother Aquinata as full of hardship because, "Needless to say, accommodations were of the most meager kind."[4] The young sisters (Borromeo was only seventeen) were traveling in full habit in a country where anti-immigrant and anti-Catholic sentiment sometimes ran high. In Traverse City, a "gruff old man"[5] took them by horse cart to a small, wooden building on the East side of Union Street between Eighth and Ninth Streets that had been purchased for them by Father Ziegler with $1,000 of his own money. The congregation supplied the sisters with $600 for furnishings for their living quarters and school. They arrived on Thursday and

Although the beginning was hard, the teaching ministry of Mother Aquinata and her followers flourished. Within two months, the student body at St. Francis had swollen from the original six to fifty. As more Catholic immigrants poured into Michigan in the boom years of the late 1800s, the demand for teaching sisters increased statewide. To meet the rising demand, Dominican sisters continued coming from New York, and eventually former pupils became sisters themselves and began to teach. Michigan, as Mother Augustine foresaw, was becoming dotted white with the habits of Dominicans.

Within four years, the sisters had started new mission schools in Bay City (St. Joseph Parish), Battle Creek

(St. Philip), and Adrian (St. Mary), and they took over a four-hundred-student school in Muskegon (St. Mary) from Immaculate Heart of Mary sisters.[6] The conditions continued to be primitive through the 1800s. Several of the sisters died of pneumonia in the harsh Michigan winters. In spite of difficulties, however, by 1885, the Dominicans had established their presence in Saginaw (St. Joseph), and at parishes in the "thumb" area of Michigan. Schools spread into mid-Michigan (Mount Pleasant, 1889) and the Leelanau area where they taught Native American students at Eagletown (Peshawbestown).[7]

High-school-aged girls at Sacred Heart Academy, founded in 1900 in Grand Rapids, learned academic subjects and such accomplishments as needlework from the sisters.

Novitiate Normal School

In 1885, the sisters in northern Michigan were given permission to create their own province when the Diocese of Grand Rapids was separated from the Detroit Diocese, which until then had included all of Michigan. In May 1886, the first postulant, Miss Josephine Gagnier (later Sister Mary Henrietta) was accepted into the newly autonomous community and began her training first under Mother Aquinata and then Novice Mistress Sister Mary Ligouri.[8] Taking the name Sister Henrietta, Gagnier learned the Native American language spoken and taught in Peshawbestown. Other young women soon joined, were trained in the religious life, and were prepared to teach in what eventually became known as Novitiate Normal School. Aquinas College claims its founding date of 1886 from the organization of that small teacher training school.

Mother Benedicta O'Rourke taught science at Sacred Heart Academy in Grand Rapids, ca. 1907.

In the 1800s, the job of Normal Schools was to train future teachers in the standards or "norms" of the regular curriculum. Though few records remain of the Novitiate Normal School's early days, typical Normal School courses included a thorough review of subject areas the student teachers were going to teach (emphasis on "the three R's"), instruction in classroom management techniques, and practice teaching in primary schools. (High school teaching, even at that time, required a college diploma in a subject area.) The Novitiate Normal School operated informally for many years before being legally incorporated in 1910. It began at Holy Angels Convent in Traverse City before moving in spring 1911 to St. John's Home on Leonard Street in Grand Rapids.[9]

There was considerable anti-Catholic bias in America at the time. Groups like the American Protective Association and Advocates of Temperance were blatantly prejudiced against Catholics. Public schools, while ostensibly nonsectarian, nonetheless included Bible reading (King James Version), Protestant hymn singing, and Protestant prayers in their school day.[10] The Catholic response, after being denied the right to read their own version of the Bible in public schools, was to build their own private education system, one that would rival or surpass the public schools in academic quality, while developing and enriching the faith of its students. Between 1880 and 1920, peak years of Catholic immigration, the number of Catholic elementary and high schools in the United States nearly doubled.

The faculty of Sacred Heart Academy included Sister Benedicta O'Rourke (second from right) and Sister Eveline Mackey (third from right) who would lead the college in its earliest years. Seated third from left is Sister Bertrand LaLonde who would later teach French at Catholic Junior College and Aquinas College.

During these years, the Novitiate Normal School flourished, graduating scores of sisters to teach in Michigan's parochial schools. Eventually, the Dominican sisters' ministry expanded into what would become Michigan's second largest city, Grand Rapids. In 1888, the sisters were called by the local bishop, Henry Joseph Richter, to come to the city to staff the first home for orphans in the western part of the state, St. John's Home. At that time, they moved their motherhouse to the comparatively cosmopolitan Furniture City, with its large population of Irish, German, and Polish furniture factory workers. The sisters incorporated in Kent County in 1892 and, as part of their charter, received authority to run "a seminary [i.e., training school for sisters] and Academy." Sacred Heart Academy opened in 1900 for local high school girls and boarders. The Novitiate Normal School, in the interim, continued to instruct the sisters in languages, the arts, science, music, and education to prepare them for their teaching careers. Bishop Richter and then his appointee Father Michael Gallagher, who also served as chaplain and spiritual director at St. John's Home, taught the sisters philosophy, Greek, and Latin. Later, Gallagher became bishop of the diocese and continued to teach the nuns.[11] Psychology and philosophy were taught by Monsignor Anthony Voelkert from St. Joseph's Seminary. The sisters also hired part-time instructors from Kalamazoo and Mount Pleasant Normal Schools for specialized courses. (These later became Western Michigan University and Central Michigan University.) By 1914, over three hundred Dominican sisters who had been trained at the Novitiate Normal School were teaching at thirty-eight parochial schools in Michigan and ran academies in Traverse City, Essexville, and Grand Rapids. In addition, they ran one central high school for girls in Grand Rapids.[12]

After World War I, Catholics began to move into the mainstream of American culture. As the need for evermore educated workers and citizens grew, the state's requirements for grade and high school teachers increased. By 1917, the Dominican sisters of Grand Rapids were reaching the limits of what the Novitiate Normal School could do. They began sending members

These Dominican sisters and three friars, pictured in 1920, completed their bachelor's degrees at the University of Notre Dame. The increasing number of sisters who needed four-year degrees eventually led to the founding of Aquinas College. Several of these sisters later joined the faculty of Catholic Junior College and Aquinas College.

of their order to Catholic University of America to receive additional teacher training. In 1918, two of the sisters received bachelor's degrees there, but the cost of sending many sisters away for additional training eventually became prohibitive. In 1919, eleven sisters passed state teacher training examinations and were certified, but new problems arose.

In those days, there was much tension around private religious education. In Michigan, the Wayne County Civic Association and the Public School Defense League pressed for a state constitutional amendment to force all Michigan students to attend public schools. This would, in effect, close all the Catholic and other denominational schools in the state. The amendment was defeated twice, but the upshot of the controversy was that the state of Michigan ratcheted up teacher requirements for *all* schools, public and parochial. This forced the sisters to increase the course offerings of the Novitiate Normal School, and then, increasingly, to send their sisters out to four-year universities (primarily Catholic University of America and the University of Notre Dame) to complete their bachelor's degrees. In 1921, sisters were even given permission to attend public universities to complete their degrees. By 1927, 56 of the sisters had earned bachelor's degrees, with nine earning master's degrees. Over 250 of the Grand Rapids Dominicans received life certificates from the state of Michigan through Central and Western State Normal Schools.[13]

Sacred Heart College

As the demand for postsecondary Catholic Education grew in the 1920s, the Novitiate Normal School grew,

All that remains of Sacred Heart College and Academy are the names inscribed in the cornice of Marywood.

too. In 1900, the sisters had established Sacred Heart Academy, a private girls' high school. The school, originally located in downtown Grand Rapids on the corner of Ransom and Fountain Streets, moved in 1922 to the newly constructed Marywood motherhouse building on East Fulton Street. (It later changed its name to Marywood Academy). Some of the girls wished to continue their education with the sisters beyond high school but to remain laywomen. So the sisters petitioned the state to open an approved teacher-training institution, Sacred Heart College, to allow young laywomen to take courses the sisters were teaching in the Novitiate Normal School. In 1922, the State of Michigan issued a charter permitting the sisters "to establish, maintain, and conduct a general college for furnishing higher learning at the City of Grand Rapids; to confer degrees and honors therefrom, and to conduct normal classes."[14]

Sacred Heart College's name was changed to Marywood College in 1927 to reflect its location at the Dominican motherhouse on Fulton Street, built in 1922.

Novitiate Normal School thus morphed into a new entity with a new name, Sacred Heart College, and admitted its first lay students, Marion McGuire, Catherine Schwaller, and one part-time student.[15] Soon, two other laywomen joined them. On June 6, 1923, Bishop Kelly and other clergy officially opened Sacred Heart College with a Solemn Pontifical High Mass. For the next nine years, laywomen students studied in postsecondary classes with the Dominican sisters. Coursework was expanded in traditional liberal arts

Dominican sisters received much of their training in summer school. During the winters, they staffed Michigan's Catholic schools. Pictured here is the faculty of the 1922 summer school.

disciplines while keeping the teacher training that had always been part of the Novitiate Normal School. Courses included philosophy, general and special methods of teaching, English, Latin, French, chemistry, physics, American and European history, algebra, geometry, and art. At the beginning, there were only five faculty members—Sisters Estelle Hackett, Jane Marie Murray, David Steele, Aquin Gallagher, and Evangelista Rohrl. The college had a small library overseen by Sister Aquin and shared facilities like classrooms and laboratories with the students of the Academy. Students who successfully completed the course work and supervised teaching experience were granted primary teaching certificates.[16]

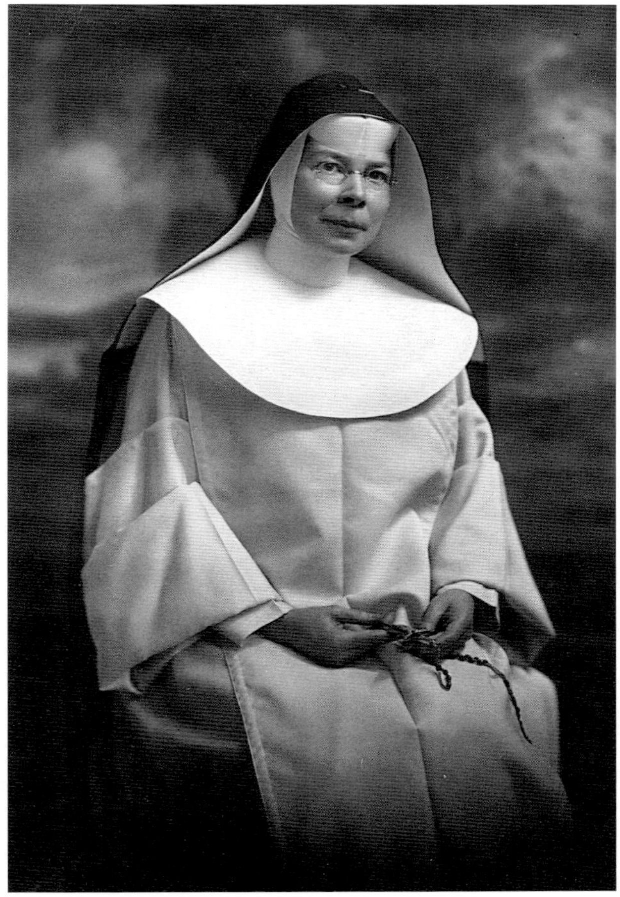

Mother Benedicta O'Rourke led Sacred Heart College in the 1920s.

Marywood College

In 1927, Sacred Heart College changed its name to Marywood College. The college advertized its location on the edge of the city as "Unsurpassed for Healthfulness and Beauty,"[17] but the campus also housed Marywood Academy, the sisters' successful girls' high school, and that led to accreditation problems. Because the high school and the college shared the name Marywood, some facilities, and some faculty, the University of Michigan balked at accepting Marywood College credits for study toward the bachelor's degree. In July 1930, Mother Benedicta O'Rourke reported to Mother Eveline Mackey, "I don't think we will receive any encouragement from Ann Arbor until we have an entirely distinctive college faculty and a complete separation of High School and College."[18]

Mother Eveline and the sisters realized that if their college was to grow and prosper, they would have to invest in a separate facility. In their General Chapter held in the summer of 1930, the members of the congregation pledged themselves to move projects forward "for the establishment of a good college for the Congregation," and they voted that each of them would attempt to earn $100 in the coming year in order to make it possible for Marywood College to buy or lease its own building in some other location.[19] Ever venturesome, Mother Eveline even set her sights on taking Marywood College to the next level by eventually making it a full-fledged junior college.

As it turned out, this desire coincided with a long-held diocesan hope to establish a Catholic junior college in Grand Rapids. As early as 1897, Bishop Richter had written to the Jesuits to ask them to establish a college in the city. Nothing came of that plan, but by 1930, the situation had changed. Traditional bachelor's degrees in those days were generally reserved for the wealthy, but as the economy changed it was clear that

THE MARYWOOD VOICE 149

Marguerite Mary Munyon — Margaret G. McCabe — Jane Mae Pidd

Mary Bernadette Brogger — Anna Marie Schmitt

Mary Frances Arehart — Marian A. Thomas — Pauline Hall

SENIOR CLASS OFFICERS

President	Marguerite Munyon
Vice President	Margaret McCabe
Secretary	Jane Mae Pidd
Treasurer	Bernadette Brogger

Novitiate Normal School evolved into Sacred Heart, then Marywood College with the admission of laywomen starting in 1922.

many workers needed more than just a high school diploma. Junior colleges filled the gap. The first one was founded in Joliet, Illinois, in 1902, and the concept proved so popular that by 1930 there were 171 public junior colleges in the United States.[20] During these same years, the number of Catholics in the United States burgeoned from 9 million to 20 million. If Catholics were to join the mainstream of American society and at the same time keep true to their heritage, they needed to build on the considerable success of their elementary and secondary schools by adding more institutions of higher education.

In spring 1931, Mother Eveline and the bishop discussed the possibility of opening such a school. The bishop was interested but requested that, if the plan were to go forward, the college be coeducational, admitting men to the previously all-female college. Things then began to move quickly. On July 3, 1931, Mother Eveline Mackey wrote a two-page letter to Bishop Joseph Pinten formally outlining her plan to take Marywood College from being a teacher-certification college to a full-fledged junior college. She realized that if this was going to happen, the enrollment of Marywood College would have to increase and it would have to have its own building. In the letter, she writes, "We believe it would be a great asset to the Catholics of Grand Rapids to have a down town [*sic*] Catholic Junior College where their sons and daughters could obtain two years of credit before leaving home for larger institutions." Anticipating even more growth, she adds, optimistically, "In due time the College could develop into a Senior College."[21] Mother Eveline proposed that the new college be located on Ransom Street, in the former home of Sacred Heart Academy. Since the Academy had been moved to the motherhouse in 1922, the old downtown building had been renamed St. Ilona Hall and had served as a residence for single working women and a school of music run by Dominican sisters. Advertising itself as "a Homey-Home for Self-supporting Girls,"[22] St. Ilona Hall was large enough to accommodate the first anticipated enrollment of students, and also had rooms for out-of-town students.

Bishop Pinten quickly approved the proposal. On Saturday, August 15, 1931, the front page of the *Grand Rapids Herald* ran a banner headline: "CATHOLIC COLLEGE WILL OPEN HERE." A smaller headline beneath the banner read, "To Be Coeducational Institution with Broad Program of Studies." The article explained that, "The chief course of study will be liberal arts. With arts and letters are to be included pre-legal and secretarial training and courses for pupils intending to go into journalism or teaching." They had only a few weeks to move Marywood College downtown, change its name, reorganize its structure, and make the old building ready for the new and returning students.

This was a tall order, but the sisters and their new dean, Dr. Burton Confrey, felt ready. It was an age of derring-do, after all. Other front-page news on that August Saturday included a story about the round-the-world flight that Charles Lindbergh and his wife were undertaking. If the Lucky Lindys could fly across the Bering Sea to Russia and China, then Marywood College could make itself Catholic Junior College in just a few weeks.

That Sunday, a letter from Bishop Pinten was read aloud at all diocesan Masses announcing the opening of Catholic Junior College. The letter reminded parishioners that Canon Law "demands that Catholic students be educated in Catholic institutions."[23] Encouraging all diocesan priests to support the new venture, the letter stated that, "The primary purpose of this college is to promote the higher education of our young men and women in accordance with Catholic principles." Other branches of knowledge would not be ignored, however. Course work would "be of the highest standard. The college will be adequately staffed and equipped to meet state requirements and the calendar and curriculum will be identical with that of the State University."[24]

And so the first institution of Catholic higher education in the country to be both coeducational and run by a congregation of religious women began. On September 28, 1931, the doors of Catholic Junior College opened on Ransom Street, and the first cohort of seventy-three students, almost evenly divided between men and women, streamed in. The college's faculty consisted of Dean Burton Confrey and eleven Dominican sisters. The tuition was fifty dollars per semester. Forty-five years after Mother Augustine's vision, the white habits of Dominic were taking another bold step into the future. It remained to be seen whether the fledgling institution could survive the deepening Depression and grow, or whether the hard economic times would end the experiment.

Endnotes

1. Quoted in Mona Schwind, O.P. *Period Pieces: An Account of the Grand Rapids Dominicans 1853–1966* (Grand Rapids, Michigan: Grand Rapids Dominicans, 1991), 22. I am indebted to Sister Mona's book for much of the early history of the Novitiate Normal School and Grand Rapids Catholic Junior College. Schwind notes that various congregations that descended from Mother Augustine's have variations of the quotation, some, including the Grand Rapids' congregation, having "peninsula" instead of "inland island" and others omit the daisy metaphor. *See* Schwind, 328. *See also* Sister Mary Philomena Kildee, O.P. *Memoirs of Mother Mary Aquinata Fiegler, O.P.* (Grand Rapids, Michigan: James Bayne Company 1928), 35.
2. *The Catholic Church in the United States.* Volume 2, (Norwood, Massachusetts: Plimpton Press, 1914), 137.
3. There is some discrepancy on the parting date of the sisters from New York. *The Catholic Church in the United States* says they left on October 22; Schwind states they left on October 15. They arrived on Thursday, October 23, 1877. Given the distance and available means of travel, I have opted for the earlier departure date.
4. Sister Mary Philomena Kildee, O.P. *Memoirs of Mother Mary Aquinata Fiegler, O.P.* (Grand Rapids, Michigan: James Bayne Company, 1928), 38.
5. Sister Mary Philip Ryan, O.P. *The Alien Corn.* (St. Charles, Illinois: Jones Wood Press, 1967), 55.
6. Schwind, 27–28.
7. Ibid., 35–36.
8. Kildee, 53.
9. Schwind, 69.
10. Rev. J. A. Burns, et al. *A History of Catholic Education in the United States* (New York: Benzeger, 1937).
11. Schwind 69–70.
12. *The Catholic Church in the United States.* 139. A boy's central high school was conducted at St. Andrew's Cathedral. These boys and girls schools eventually merged into Catholic Central High School.
13. Schwind, 101–102.
14. Sister Marjorie Vangsness, O.P., "History of Certification with the Michigan State Department of Education." Aquinas College Archives.
15. Schwind, 108.
16. Mother Benedicta, O.P., correspondence. Letter of November 10, 1924. Marywood Archives.
17. *The Marywood Voice.* Vol. 1, Number 1. October 1927.
18. Quoted in Schwind, 175.
19. Schwind, 175.
20. J. A. Birns. *A History of Catholic Education in the United States: A Textbook for Normal Schools and Teacher Colleges.* NYU: Benzeger, 1937.
21. Mother Eveline Mackey, O.P., correspondence. Marywood Archives.
22. *The Marywood Voice,* Vol. 1, Number 1. 1927.
23. Bishop Joseph Pinten, Letter. Diocese of Grand Rapids Chancery Office. August 11, 1931.
24. Ibid.

Chapter 2

Catholic Junior College 1931–1940

Founding Catholic Junior College was a risk. Money was hard to come by, and the economic forecast was dim. The country was one year into the Great Depression, and unemployment nationwide was 16 percent and rising. To become fully accredited, the small school would have to convince major four-year schools, like the Universities of Michigan and Notre Dame, to accept its credits. In spite of these potential roadblocks, Mother Eveline and the faculty were undaunted. Their purpose and mission were clear.

Dr. Burton Confrey, the first dean of the college, explained the essentially Catholic mission of the school in the August 1931 *Grand Rapids Herald* story that announced the new school's opening. He stated that Catholic philosophy would inform all course work, and there would be specially focused Catholic courses like Catholic Action and theology "to give students correct ethical standards and the right outlook on life." He added, "All instruction will prepare them for a normal Christian life, in whatever vocation divine Providence directs." Articulating the purpose of the college further, he said, "Catholic Junior College is not just another college. . . . for here the course in religion, which aims to build good character on which to base solidly supernatural virtue, is the very core of the whole curriculum. It is a dynamic institution housing an energetic attempt to inculcate in our young men and women Christian principles which if widely accepted, would save American family life, the basis of our national life and of Christian civilization."

The academic course work would be rigorous. Confrey said each course would have four objectives: knowledge of the particular field of study, knowledge of literature in the field, the ability to conduct research in that field, and the ability to think in that field. "To help students develop these objectives, classes will be conducted so as to give the maximum practice in discussion, criticism, and application."[1]

The original Catholic Junior College building stood at the corner of Ransom and Fountain Streets in downtown Grand Rapids.

The visionary leadership of Mother Eveline Mackey guided the transformation of Marywood College into Catholic Junior College (1931) then Aquinas College (1940). Catholic Junior College was the first Catholic coeducational college in the United States to be run by a congregation of religious women.

The transformation from Marywood College to Catholic Junior College was not without its difficulties. The bishop and the congregation struggled over the issue of ownership and control, a controversy that eventually would require an appeal to Rome for clarification. Some early documents refer to the college as a diocesan institution while Mother Eveline Mackey and the sisters insisted that it was a Dominican institution located in the Diocese of Grand Rapids, but otherwise it was, by rights, independent of the bishop. These issues were important because of questions of who controlled the academic program and who could hire and release faculty and staff. At least once, the bishop tried to prevent the sisters from rehiring certain faculty members, but the sisters resisted. They wanted to maintain control of the college so that it could pursue its academic program in the way they felt would best serve the needs of the students and college. Eventually, a letter from Rome stated that the sisters, as Dominicans, were papally instituted and not under the direct jurisdiction of the local bishop. They could, therefore, run their college as a legally separate entity from the diocese. By the time this matter was ironed out, both Bishop Pinten and Mother Eveline were dead, but at last the college and the diocese knew where they stood. The college and the bishops who have succeeded Bishop Pinten have maintained a cordial and special relationship ever since, and, especially in the early years, the college drew its student body largely from the Grand Rapids Diocese, which includes almost all of western Michigan. Over the ensuing years, the local bishops have participated in campus life, presiding at the dedication of buildings, at Baccalaureate Masses and other campus liturgical events.

The Academic Program

The 1935–36 catalog states:

As a Catholic institution of learning, Catholic Junior College addresses itself to the important work of forming the youth under its charge into educated men and women of deep practical faith. It has, then, a twofold purpose: first, the intellectual development, and secondly, the moral-religious training of future lay leaders of the church. Since religion is a field of knowledge as well as a life to be lived, the courses in religion constitute an integral, not merely added, part of the curriculum. They also serve to give the intellectual basis of moral and religious life.[2]

The tone and ethos of the college was set early by Dean Confrey. Confrey, who had taught at both Catholic University of America and the University of Notre Dame, was a published fiction writer, and he brought a poet's sensitivity to the early years of the school. In 1933, as the first two-year students completed their education, Confrey decided there would not be a traditional commencement ceremony. Rather, he turned to an older tradition. On the night before commencement, graduating students held vigil "to recover the ideals of knighthood." The night was spent "in meditation on the solemnity of the milestone reached and the responsibility of the candidate for knighthood as a Christian soldier."[3]

In addition to religion courses, the curriculum emphasized the liberal arts more than most junior colleges. Catholic Junior College's course offerings included English, foreign languages, mathematics, science, and history. Career-oriented programs included journalism, pre-law, pre-medical, pre-engineering, pre-business administration, teacher training, nursing, and music. Individual courses ran the gamut from accounting to zoology. Sciences like botany, chemistry, and physics took their place beside music, philosophy, and religion. The religion offerings included "Dogmatics 1 and 2," "Religion for Nurses," and "Teaching of Religion." (The college proclaimed itself open to "persons of all creeds" and so, in sensitivity to their beliefs, non-Catholic students were exempted from both the religion course requirements and also religious activities such as the annual retreat.)[4]

The entire staff consisted of Father Arthur Bukowski, who had been appointed dean and chaplain by Bishop Pinten in 1934 when Confrey left, twenty-three sisters, and three lay faculty. Sisters in the upper administration included Sister Martin Fehan, assistant to the dean; Sister Felix Brand, registrar; Sister Malachi Laithwaite, librarian; and Sister Agnes Marie Flohe, treasurer. According to college legend, Sister Agnes Marie literally kept the finances of the college in a cigar box. (No word of who had smoked the cigars!)

Catholic Junior College graduating class of 1935. The sisters had a separate graduation ceremony, usually at the end of the summer session.

Catholic Junior College graduating class of 1938. Father Arthur Bukowski, the college's first president, sits center, first row.

like Olivet, Calvin, Gonzaga, and St. Mary's.[5] The close quarters and small student body led to a strong sense of community among the faculty, staff, and students, so much so that in 1981, fifty years after the opening of the college, Aquinas College hosted a Catholic Junior College reunion that drew more than fifty people, nearly a quarter of those who had ever graduated from the school.

The Dominican sisters, knowing that the integrity of their new college would depend on the academic credentials of the faculty, sent Sisters Mildred Hawkins and Bertrand LaLonde to European universities to earn doctorates in classical studies and French, respectively. In 1938, Sister Bertrand was awarded the Prix de Langue Francaise by the French government for her doctoral work on the French novelist, academician, and politician Maurice Barres. She went on to teach French at Catholic Junior College and Aquinas College for over thirty years.

The student body in the mid-1930s totaled about 90 students at any given time, and in its history CJC graduated about 226 men and women with two-year degrees. An article in *Michigan Catholic* on November 11, 1937, reported that 60 percent of the graduates of Catholic Junior College went on to pursue four-year bachelor's degrees at large institutions such as DePaul University, University of Detroit, the University of Michigan, the University of Notre Dame, Central State, Michigan State, and smaller liberal arts schools

The entire college, except for the music program, was housed in a nineteenth-century red brick building at 69 Ransom Street SE (the current site of the main branch of the Grand Rapids Public library's parking lot). The four-story building held two offices, four classrooms, four laboratories, a library, three restrooms and a chapel. When the entire college needed to congregate for assemblies, they met at the Knights of Columbus Hall across the street. Physical education classes were offered at Grand Rapids Junior College, just a walk uphill from the Ransom Street building. The Music Department, headed by Sister Thomas McNamara, had its classes and studios in a small house near the main building.

Ireland-born Sister Malachi Laithewaite, Catholic Junior College's librarian, was an acquaintance of C. S. Lewis, Beatrix Potter, and J. R. R. Tolkein, and served as the college librarian.

In the hardscrabble Depression years, everyone pulled together to make

Pictured in the library with students, Father Arthur Bukowski, dean of Catholic Junior College from 1934, was named president in 1937.

Catholic Junior College work. Tuition was set at $50 per semester, but in light of the times, Dean Bukowski briefly lowered the tuition to $30 to make it possible for more students to attend. (That noble gesture had to be rescinded soon). The college was a bootstraps operation, and Father Bukowski and the sisters made ample use of work-study money, funded by the National Recovery Act, to employ student workers as library staff, janitors, and maintenance men. Faculty members, including Father Bukowski, were actively involved in recruiting students. Alumnus Casimir Razmus recalled that after he graduated from Catholic Central High School in the 1930s, Father Bukowski came to his door and asked him if he wanted to go to college. He did, but his family had no money. Father Bukowski offered him a job, and for the next two years, while taking classes, he and other students scraped old wallpaper and paint from the walls, cleaned hallways, and stoked the boiler in winter in exchange for tuition.[6]

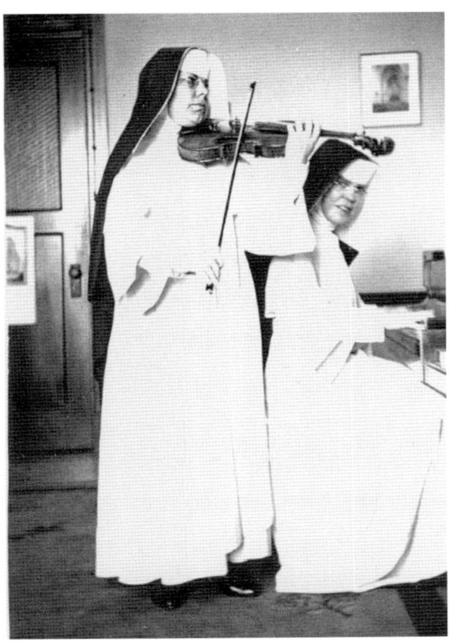

Sisters Margaret Ann Kaiser and Denise Suprenant practice music at CJC's St. Ann's Hall.

Eventually word of Catholic Junior College began to spread outside the Grand Rapids area. Students from other parts of Michigan where Dominican sisters taught began arriving for classes. Local students came to campus by foot, car, bus, or bicycle, while out-of-town first-year women were housed in a small dormitory on the fourth floor of the classroom building. Sophomores roomed in Esther Hall, a Heritage Hill residence run by the Methodist Church, and young male students found approved apartment lodgings in the downtown area.

The faculty of Catholic Junior College consisted almost entirely of Dominican sisters.

Student Life

Even though academic regulations were strict, the students of Catholic Junior College found time for approved—and unapproved—extracurricular activities. A *Michigan Catholic* article about the college reports,

Basketball became CJC's first organized sport. Here the 1939 roundball squad poses with Coach Ed White.

"Extra-curricular life plays a dominant part in the Catholic Junior College scheme. It is looked upon as a laboratory in which the fundamental teachings of the college are put into place. In view of the increasing importance of leisure time, it is of the greatest importance that the students learn the proper method of employing their time outside of working hours, and here, too, the students find full scope to put into practice the Christian principles which [their] education aims to implant in [their] nature."

As a two-year school, the Junior College Raiders played other college's freshmen or junior varsity teams.

Among the college-sanctioned activities were the Catholic Life Conference, whose role was to oversee activities and insure that they aligned themselves with Catholic practice and ideals; the Catholic Evidence Club, which discussed religious issues; and the Women's Club and Men's Club. *Le Cercle Francais* gave students a chance to brush up their French language skills, and the Secretarial Club and Music Clubs gave students a chance to improve their abilities in shorthand and music performance.

The only intercollegiate sport during those early years was basketball. Since the college was only a two-year school, the team found itself playing the freshman teams of four-year colleges like Calvin. Because they had to practice at the city-run Junior College gymnasium, the team had to be up at odd hours, between six and seven in the morning. In the early years, there were only six players on the team, and when they had road games to Hope College, the entire team crammed into one car. All other sports were intramural until baseball was added as a second sport later in the 1930s. The goal of the sports program was "to foster a spirit of union, sportsmanship and loyalty, and contribute to bodily health."[7] The sports activities were governed by the Catholic Junior College Athletic Association.

Baseball became CJC's second sport.

Faculty member John Bellardo (left) relaxes with students.

Many of these activities were reported on by the campus newspaper, *The Lantern*, started in 1933 and produced bimonthly on mimeograph by students Joe Murphy and John McDuffee, who later went on to become priests in the Grand Rapids Diocese. By 1936, this shoestring operation was replaced by a regular tabloid-format newspaper called the *Catholic Junior Herald*, overseen by Sister Aquin Gallagher. In addition to the run of normal college activities, the *Herald* reported on local and regional news and Catholic Action rallies.

The Depression years forced students to become self-reliant when it came to other activities. Like students in all generations, they were inventive. Dr. Confrey, in the earliest years of the college, set aside one room on the first floor of the Ransom Street building as a study room for men. According to alumnus Joe Cavera, the male scholars were more apt to go in there to smoke cigarettes and play hearts. When the dean would rap on the locked door and ask "Is there a fire in there?," the students would open the windows and crawl onto the long back porch of the Ransom Street building to finish their cigarettes before the dean returned with the room key. Cavera also remembers a farm boy from Parnell who would sneak a flask of home-brewed corn whiskey into the coatroom where students who dared could have a hair-raising clandestine drink.[8]

According to Catholic Junior College alumni, the social life was free and easy. The small cadre of students partied together, and on Ascension Day each year the college sponsored a college picnic. The Women's Club sponsored an annual hike, and students staged amateur theatricals. St. Cecilia Auditorium became the scene of a 1938 variety revue called "Campus Silhouettes" full of satirical skits and songs, demonstrations of ballroom dances, and a ladies' style show.

Students in the 1930s enjoyed an annual picnic at Johnson Park.

Transition

As Catholic Junior College continued to prosper, Sister Mildred Hawkins, academic dean, was anxious for the school to expand into a third and fourth year and become a bachelor's degree granting college. Father Arthur Bukowski was more conservative and, at first, resisted the change, fearing the financial risk. But Sisters Mildred and Jerome Smithers, both strong women, pushed the idea forward. Late in life, Bukowski admitted he had been too hesitant in those days. "I should have gone out on a limb more than I did," he said in an interview a few years before he died.[9]

The move toward a four-year college began as early as 1936, prompted when the State Department of Education raised its requirements for teacher certification. Since so many of the Catholic Junior College students intended to go into teaching, this forced the need for many of them to take a third year of courses beyond the two-year college degree. Since so many of the students were sisters, the Dominican congregation was finding it increasingly expensive to send them away to large universities to complete their certification requirements and degrees. In October 1936, Catholic Junior College representatives drove to Lansing to meet with a Mr. Emens, the state's director of teacher certification, to discuss adding a third year to the curriculum. Emens informed them that could not be done unless the college was first recognized by the North Central Association of Colleges. After some discussion, Emens agreed to accept fifteen semester hours from the college toward renewal of teacher certification *provided that* three colleges or universities to which the sisters would transfer for bachelor's degrees would accept the credits. He recommended that rather than take these classes at Catholic Junior College, however, the sisters take them via correspondence courses from large universities. This idea was not at all satisfactory to the directors of the Junior College, but they returned to Grand Rapids and eventually got the University of Notre Dame, the University of Detroit, and Marygrove College to accept the additional fifteen credits from CJC. Two years later, however, Notre Dame changed its position and decided not to accept credits earned by correspondence courses. The college seemed at an impasse.

The Catholic Junior College Women's League took a hike each spring.

The Board of Trustees in those years was the leadership of the Dominican congregation. To make the Junior College more closely resemble a four-year college, Mother Euphrasia Sullivan in 1937 gained the North Central Board's approval to promote Father Bukowski from dean to president, which he remained until his retirement in 1968.[10]

In the summer of 1938, a visitation team that included Mr. Emens; Dr. George Carothers, president of the Michigan Association of North Central Colleges; and a Dr. Williams, assistant registrar of the University of Michigan, came to campus and visited classes. Carothers was encouraging, saying that a third year would be feasible if the college could expand its faculty, course offerings, and library. Accordingly, in spring 1939, Catholic Junior College announced that it would begin offering a third year of course work the following year. Later that summer, a group of eight faculty came from the University of Michigan to review the academic program for the North Central Association, with an eye to accreditation. Things looked promising.

The matter was hardly settled, however. Mr. Emens, who had been involved in the case since 1936, was replaced by a new director of certification in Lansing, a Dr. Tidrick, a martinet when it came to precise standards and paperwork. Approval for the fourth year was put on hold, and the college's plans were threatened to be overwhelmed by state bureaucracy. Another year of wrangling with the state took place, involving not only Catholic Junior College but other local Catholic institutions of education as well, and then, in May 1940, the Michigan Association of North Central Colleges issued its official report on Catholic Junior College's status: certification as a four-year school was approved!

Only one more thing was required. The two-year Catholic Junior College needed a name change to denote its new four-year status. In the summer of 1940, the sisters decided to christen their new venture "Aquinas College" to honor both their original mother superior, Sister Aquinata Fiegler, and the greatest philosopher of the Middle Ages, the Dominican St. Thomas Aquinas.

Articles of incorporation were filed in Lansing on January 16, 1941, and the college community eagerly looked forward to growth. The fledgling school had weathered the worst years of the Great Depression and had prospered, but new challenges lay ahead. As the newly named Aquinas College began this phase of its life, the economic depression was not over, Europe was plunged in the midst of a horrific war whose outcome was unclear, and, unbeknownst to anyone, the Japanese attack on Pearl Harbor was less than eleven months away.

Endnotes

1. *The Grand Rapids Herald*, August 15, 1931, 1–2.
2. 1935–36 college catalog, 4.
3. Catholic Junior College press release printed in *Michigan Catholic*, May 18, 1933.
4. *Michigan Catholic*, September 1, 1933.
5. *Michigan Catholic*, November 11, 1937, 31.
6. Aquinas College Historical Commission, *Historically Speaking*, disc 1. (1997).
7. *Michigan Catholic*, November 11, 1937, 31+.
8. *Historically Speaking*, disc 1.
9. *Historically Speaking*, disc 1.
10. Schwind, 233.

Chapter 3

Years of Transition 1940–1954

In June 1940, Catholic Junior College's final class graduated. A few weeks later, summer courses began at the newly named Aquinas College. Enrollment in the 1940s would eventually swell to 665 full- and part-time students necessitating the purchase of two apartment buildings on Ransom Street for residences for the sisters and female students. The faculty consisted of seventeen sisters, two priests, and six lay faculty who were paid the princely salary of $1,600 per year. (Tuition was $50 per semester.) Before the fledgling college could get its proper footing, however, America's involvement in World War II intervened.

The War Years

Throughout 1940 and 1941, the pages of the *Aquinas Herald* were filled with editorials arguing both for and against the United States getting involved in the European and Pacific war that had started in September of 1939. After Pearl Harbor, though, the debate stopped. America was at war with Japan, Germany and its allies, and the faculty and students of Aquinas stepped up to do their part. In October 1942, a joint Army-Navy-Marine recruiting board visited campus, and students enlisted, led by Carl Absmeier, Class of '43, who joined the Army Air Corps. Dorothy Joseffy became the first Aquinas female student to join the WACS.[1] (They had been preceded in the service by aviation cadet Bonnie O'Brien, '36, who was killed in an air crash before Pearl Harbor.)[2] Faculty members Thomas T. Murphy, Thomas Neill, and John Oesterle left the college to go into the service. Murphy later fought at Guadalcanal and in the Solomon Islands. The college's doctor, John Whalen, joined the Army. Former student Vete Bartnick joined the Polish squadron of Britain's Royal Air Force and was killed in a bomber crash.[3]

War news mingled with stories of campus life in the *Aquinas Herald* whose pages were filled with news items and photographs of Aquinas's service men and women. A 1943 story, for example, told about

Even though the Robinson Road campus was occupied after 1945, graduation ceremonies continued to be held downtown at the Knights of Columbus Hall across the street from the Ransom Street campus. This 1949 view looks up Library Street towards Division Avenue.

In December 1944, students Edmund Kieras and Betty Butler check out Aquinas College's World War II service flag. Six Aquinas students were killed while serving in World War II.

Lenore Fisher, Class of '41, who was serving with the Women's Army Air corps as a mapmaker. Students left on the home front did their part to support the war effort. They collected pennies for copper salvage, sold war stamps and bonds, and held regular prayer sessions and Masses for the troops. In 1942, Aquinas College bested the other colleges in Grand Rapids by collecting more money per capita—eighty-nine cents—than the other schools in the annual December War Chest competition.

In November 1942, the college dedicated a service flag. Mother Euphrasia Sullivan, Father Bukowski, faculty, and students displayed the flag that honored the 116 Aquinas students and faculty then in the military. In addition to current students, all five male graduates of the first Aquinas College graduating class (1942) were in the service, according to the *Aquinas Herald* story that covered the flag raising. Blue stars represented active service personnel and gold stars represented those killed in action. By the end of the war, the Aquinas service flag would have 273 blue stars and six gold. A wartime curriculum was added to regular courses, with the inclusion of an aviation course, first-aid training, and bacteriology, chemistry, and physics courses specially designed for nurses and naval reservists. Towards the end of the war, a special forty-week course called the Polish Seminar was instituted with the intention of sending volunteers to aid recovery efforts in war-ravaged Poland when the war was over. Students were required to speak Polish to enroll in the program, and they then received training in the skills they would need to rebuild the country. Seven students completed the seminar and were prepared to go to Poland to work with the Bishops' Committee for Polish Relief, but the postwar occupation of Poland by the Soviet Union and the subsequent Cold War made that impossible.

Despite the serious decline in the number of male students in the early war years, the college tried to carry on life as usual, but the war was never far away. In late fall 1942, male students who had enlisted in the reserves were notified that they should not enroll for second semester classes as they were about to be called into active service. In January, the student newspaper announced that the 1943 prom, scheduled for May, was being moved to February because of "the exigencies of war," and a few days after the dance thirteen Army reservists were called to active duty. Ken Marin, then a student and later an Aquinas economics professor, recalled, "All the remaining Aquinas reservists were called out to duty, and we marched down to the bus station and were sent off to Fort Custer [in Battle Creek], and that morning there was a big sendoff with virtually the whole student body because we were all part of that student body ourselves."[4] (Male student enrollment dropped from sixty-four in 1942-43 to only fifteen in 1943-44.) The young soldiers, sailors, fliers, and marines could not have known as they climbed on the bus, but their quick and unexpected call-up was part of the preparation for D-Day, only a few months away.

The 1944 prom featured students in uniform who were about to be called into active duty.

After the war was over, many students, like Marin, returned to civilian life and completed their degrees thanks to the GI Bill. They did not forget their fallen comrades, however. In the years after the war, the veterans themselves took up a collection, raised $2,000, and personally constructed the shrine to Our Lady of Fatima. Dedicated in May 1950, the shrine stands on the east side of the Holmdene lawn as a memorial to those members of the Aquinas community who died in World War II.

A Four-Year College

The first graduates of Aquinas College received their bachelor's degrees on May 26, 1942. The five men and three women had taken their first two years of courses at Catholic Junior College and their second two at Aquinas College. Dr. Jerome Kerwin of the University of Chicago was the commencement speaker at St. Cecilia Auditorium, just across the street from the Ransom Street campus. There had been a Baccalaureate Mass the previous Sunday at Marywood.

Relationships among the faculty, staff, and students were close in those early years. Class sizes were small, sometimes as small as two or three students, and all the functions of the college, except for music classes, were housed in the Ransom Street building. The college hired more lay faculty in those years, retaining the services of John Bellardo, mathematics and sciences, who was described by one former student as a man who was both shy and brusque. Added to the faculty were Thomas Murphy, who taught commerce; John Oesterle,

Returning G.I.'s filled postwar classrooms with students like Ken Marin (second from left) who later became an economics professor at Aquinas College. Seated third from left is Mildred de Alva, later Marin's wife.

Father Gary teaches an evening class in theology at the Ransom Street campus, 1948. Day classes had been moved to the recently purchased Robinson Road campus.

a philosophy professor; and Dorothy Kardes, physical education. Dr. Thomas Neill taught at the college and acted as dean of men for a few years before leaving for military service and a subsequent career with St. Louis University. Their annual salaries varied between $1,600 and $2,200, and some were expected to staff the college's extension programs in Saginaw and later in Muskegon.[5]

The majority of the faculty members were Dominican sisters whom former students remembered with a mixture of fondness and awe. Chemistry instructor Sister Mark Scanlon, who was a somewhat diminutive nun, nonetheless was capable of striking fear in her students with her beginning of the semester announcement that half of them would likely be gone from the course by the end of the term. Sister Marcelline Horton, a botanist, was an authority on Michigan orchids, and Sister Gonzaga Udell is remembered as a strict grammarian. The Music Department was staffed by Sister Thomas McNamara and Sister Evangelista Rohrl, offering instruction in piano, composition, and voice. Sister Bertrand LaLonde, who had earned her Ph.D. in France, taught her French students to speak so well that at least one serviceman, Bill Alexander, later commented that when he was in service during the war the French people he met complimented him on the quality of his accent.

President Bukowski's annual reports list the professional activities of faculty who, even in these early years, were presenting scholarly papers at national conferences. Enrollment swelled during the 1940s, from 601 full- and part-time students near the beginning of the decade to 1,074 at its end. The vast majority of graduates were in the liberal arts. Because the Dominican sisters who were in training were needed to teach in the Catholic schools around Michigan, most of them attended Aquinas College's large summer sessions and graduated in August, some of them taking many years to complete their bachelor's degrees. During the fall and winter semesters, classrooms were filled with many more lay students than religious. A music bachelor's degree was added in 1944, as was a major in sociology, Father Bukowski's field.

The teaching sisters provided encouragement and sometimes maternal care for the students. Helen Imperi Alexander, who with her husband Bill became probably the first Aquinas students to marry each other, recalled that she dropped out of school in her third year when she got married and subsequently became pregnant. While Bill was gone to war and Helen was living with her parents as she awaited the birth of their first child, Sister Aquin Gallagher personally called on her and persuaded her to return to school to finish her last semester. Wearing her husband's large jackets to modestly cover her pregnancy, Helen came back to classes and finished her degree, and she credits Sister Aquin. That is exactly the kind of academic and personal encouragement that many Aquinas students remember from those early years.

The Dominican sisters who taught and administered the college were ahead of their time in many ways. In an age when it was unusual for women to earn college degrees, they became college professors, attended professional academic conferences, and earned advanced degrees both here in the United States and abroad. The result was that they became role models for the laywomen students and for the younger sisters under their tutelage. As Sister Mona Schwind points out in *Period Pieces*:

As religious women-scholars, they served as role models for women and contributed to the formation of candidates within the congregation. While the greatest number of women in the congregation taught children and youth, the college faculty was necessarily involved in adult education and in the preparation of lay leadership in the Church. Tenure in their college roles provided the college community with a stability which other sisters did not customarily have. As a result, the "college nuns" came to have an acknowledged leadership in policy making and in intellectual and spiritual development of the congregation.[6]

As the college grew in the 1940s, the Dominican sisters and lay faculty were joined by Dominican priests like Father Leo Arnault from the University of Notre Dame, who taught Thomistic philosophy until 1949. Fathers B. Urban Fay, Martin Gary, and William Tarrier both taught and served as chaplains for the college, deans of men, athletic coaches, and advisors for student programs. Like the sisters, they provided an ongoing pastoral presence on campus and students interacted with them both in their professorial and their priestly capacities.

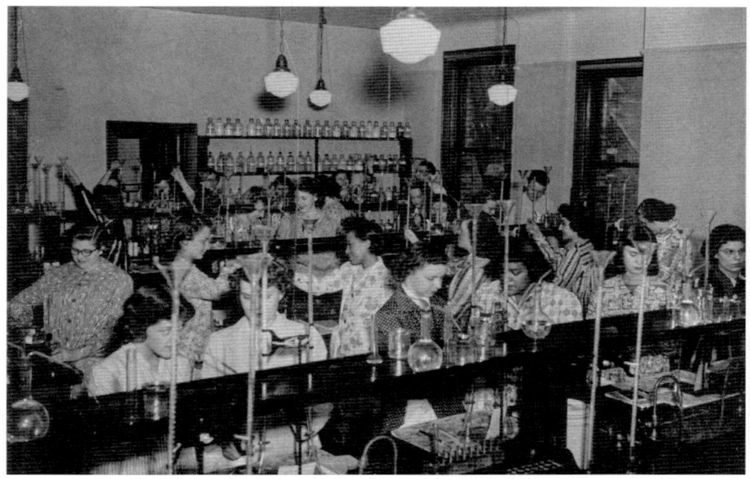

The crowded laboratories on the Ransom Street campus served Aquinas College science students as well as these St. Mary's nursing students.

The academic program included a large liberal arts component, with upwards of seventy credit hours required in general education in addition to the courses required for the major. Students could major in modern languages, English, history, and other liberal arts disciplines. Areas of professional training included accounting, business, education, pre-engineering, and secretarial science. Library holdings were crammed into one room in the Ransom Street building, but students regularly made use of the Ryerson Library, the main branch of the Grand Rapids Public Library, right next door. The Aquinas Library and the Public Library maintained a good relationship, with the college librarian sorting out the Grand Rapids Public Library books that students returned by mistake.

In 1941, feeling some growing pains, the college acquired two more buildings on Library Street. The purchase of the former Closterhouse Apartments virtually doubled the space of the college. Though the buildings were not very attractive, they gave the college room for residences for the sisters, an expanded library, and a chapel that sat up to eighty people. Fifteen women students were housed on the top floor. The resident students took their meals in the dining room of Father Bukowski's nearby house. The space cleared in the original building was converted into rooms for the Women's League, the Men's Union, the *Aquinas Herald*, and a common room.

Male students attempt a human pyramid on the downtown campus.

Student activities continued as they had at Catholic Junior College with many of the activities centered on the Catholic faith, including the Catholic Life Conference, to which most students belonged. That group later changed its name to the Student Guild. Special commemoration was made of the feast of St. Thomas Aquinas on March 7, and that day, after 1943, became known as Academic Day, an annual event which students from area Catholic high schools also attended. The first formal rosary procession, which became an annual event for many years on the campus, was held on October 18, 1945, and the first Marian Congress was held in May 1947.

Academic life was enriched by a monthly program of speakers. Such mid-twentieth century luminaries as Mortimer Adler, Baroness Catherine de Hueck, Dorothy Day, and many well-known Catholic theologians and philosophers spoke at Aquinas-sponsored events held at the Knights of Columbus Hall, the Ladies Literary Club, or the St. Cecilia Auditorium. One especially memorable visit was in December 1944. The von Trapp family singers, well known even before their story got told in *The Sound of Music,* were performing in Grand Rapids, and the baron, baroness, their children, and their chaplain dined with Father Bukowski and students at Father Bukowski's residence.

Father Bukowski's strong social service ethic led the campus to reach out into the community. In 1938, he founded a "Center for Negro Instruction" which eventually was renamed after the Dominican Saint Martin de Porres. Meeting at the St. Vincent de Paul Society on Grandville Avenue, the Martin de Porres Center enlisted speakers and entertainers to provide education and enrichment for residents of the inner city every Wednesday of the school year. In addition, the college sponsored a Vacation School for Children,

The von Trapp Family Singers dined with Monsignor Bukowski in December 1944 while in Grand Rapids. Maria is third from the left seated. Her husband Georg sits beside Father Bukowski.

and in May 1942 a second center was opened on Logan Street to provide services, instruction, and entertainment six nights a week. So strong was the college's general commitment to service, that history professor Lewis Clingman and his wife Dorothy lived at Augustine House, as the center was known, and ran the programs.[7] Among students, the Interracial Justice Club flourished during this period.

In 1945, Aquinas College purchased property at 1607 Robinson Road that included the stately Holmdene mansion built by Edward Lowe in 1908.

Throughout the years of his tenure as president, Father (later Monsignor) Bukowski inspired the members of the campus community to serve the world, whether it was in early interfaith dialogs with Temple Emmanuel's Rabbi Jerome Folkman, ecumenical discussions with members of west Michigan's Protestant communities or taking students to Appalachia on service trips. He was an early leader in improving race relations in America, serving as vice president of the Michigan Committee on Civil Rights and chair of the Grand Rapids chapter in the early 1950s. He was a frequent speaker locally and regionally on Catholic Higher Education. Graduates from those years remember Bukowski as a spiritual presence on campus and off. In addition to being president of the college and teaching sociology, he regularly came to the meetings of student organizations to share his wisdom and spirit.

Robinson Road

As World War II drew to a close, Aquinas readied itself for its next great leap. Anticipating that peacetime veterans would swell enrollment, the Dominican sisters who formed the governing board of the college decided to take another bold step. Realizing the landlocked Ransom Street campus would be too small, they decided to find a campus that would look and feel like a traditional college campus. In 1945, the opportunity arose.

The Dominican leadership and members of the college had for some time been looking at a parcel of property not far from the Marywood motherhouse. The land, the former estate of lumber baron Edward Lowe and his wife, came up for sale after Edward's death in the late 1930s. At that time, the sisters considered the asking price too high, and Bishop Pinten and M. E. Davenport both went after the property. The bishop wished to transfer the location of St. John's Home, and the Lowe heirs even petitioned township officials for a zoning variance to allow the orphanage to relocate there. At the same time, Davenport, an educator, wished to open a business school there, to be called the University of Grand Rapids. As it turned out, Davenport got the nod from estate executor James Lowe, and the for-profit University of Grand Rapids opened its doors and began holding classes on the former estate.

The university was short-lived, however. Even though it had established itself as a college and even had a football team (whose assistant coach was a recent University of Michigan graduate and football player, Gerald R. Ford), it couldn't sustain the sudden exit of its largely male student body when the Second World War broke out. The university folded and had to abandon the campus. (The financially reorganized university is now known as Davenport University.)

When the Robinson Road campus was purchased in 1945, students pitched in to clear the neglected and overgrown property.

Perhaps it wasn't just the sudden decline in students that spelled the end of the University of Grand Rapids, however. A precious piece of Aquinas folklore says that after the sisters initially lost the property because it cost too much, the formidable Sister Mildred Hawkins, the college's academic dean, secretly buried religious medals on the University of Grand Rapids campus. She bided her time, asked the college community to pray for a special intention, and shortly thereafter the long-desired property became available—and at a price the Dominican leadership felt the college could afford.[8] The sisters moved quickly. Mother Euphrasia first learned the property was for sale on April 17, 1945. Within five days, she and Sister Joachim met with Bishop Francis J. Haas (who had succeeded long-serving Bishop Pinten), who then made a site visit to the campus and gave his assent to the purchase, though he was wary of the $150,000 price tag. Acting on the bishop's advice, the Dominican leadership contacted Edward Frey and Michael Leonard, who were officials of the Union Bank of Michigan and also members of the college's Lay Advisory Board. Permission for the sisters to go into debt was hurriedly requested from and agreed to by the Holy See, and by April 25 the sisters had secured a $115,000 loan to purchase the sixty-seven acres and its buildings for the college's new campus. Father Bukowski announced the news to the college community at an assembly the next day, and the day following that the *Grand Rapids Herald* ran the headline, "Aquinas College Buys University of G.R. Site."[9]

Included in the purchase were several historic buildings, including the Lowe's English Renaissance style manor house, the stables, a small winery, and a carriage house, all of which would be put to use for the business of the college. For the time being, the college would operate two campuses, the old one on Ransom Street and the new campus on the then-outskirts of the city. Plans were made to expand the number of buildings on campus by taking on major construction of an administration and classroom building, but, at a cost of almost half a million dollars, those plans would have to wait ten years. In the meantime, students were recruited to scythe down the long grass that had grown up on the property in the time between the University of Grand Rapids' closing and Aquinas's purchase of the land. The old stable would be renovated in 1946 for use as a gymnasium, and Holmdene, the stately building constructed in 1908, was destined to become both an administrative center and classroom building. A Men's Union was created in the basement, and the third-floor ballroom found a new use as the college's chapel. Classes were held on the second floor.

During the summer of 1945, the sisters of Marywood, Father Bukowski, and the janitor Mr. McDonald prepared the campus to receive its first students come September. The following spring, the North Central Association approved Aquinas College as a fully accredited four-year college, and Aquinas began to grow into its new home. The influx of war veterans swelled enrollment to 564 by the fall of 1947, and the college began to attract small numbers of foreign students from as far away as China and Nigeria.

In the spring of 1945, an unsigned reminiscence appeared in the *Aquinas Herald* from a member of the last class to graduate from the Ransom Street campus:

We seniors are happy that Aquinas has at last acquired physical facilities to match its high quality of instruction. At the same time, we are glad that we will graduate from the old building. We are the stragglers of an old tradition. We belong to a time when Aquinas cheered itself with the classic statement of the requirements for a university—a capable teacher at one end of a log and an interested student at the other end. We have been sitting on a log so long that we would feel out of place in an easy chair. . . .

We didn't need modern buildings and landscaped grounds, we kept telling ourselves and everyone outside the college. But we talked about the day when we would buy the Ryerson Library and turn the YMCA into a dormitory and Fulton Park into our south campus. . . .

Many of our old traditions will continue. Others will be outmoded and replaced by new ones. As the transplanted Aquinas flourishes, the Class of 1945 will rejoice. But we will still take pride in saying, "We were Aquinas when it was just a struggling institution in a time-scarred building, and had nothing to recommend it except the finest students and faculty that ever studied and worked and played together.[10]

On November 6, 1945, Bishop Haas, Father Bukowski, and other dignitaries officially blessed the new campus and prayerfully inaugurated a new era in the college's history. Three years later, in his annual report, Bukowski reflected that it had been twenty-five years since that day in 1922 when the sisters opened the doors of Sacred Heart College to laywomen. "No ceremony marked the twenty-fifth anniversary," he wrote, "The growth during this time has been rather remarkable, but the college prefers to look to the future with anticipation of greater service."[11]

The Fabulous Fifties

For the next ten years, Aquinas College's downtown campus remained the site for science labs, music classes, and night courses while the Robinson Road campus became home to liberal arts courses. Students and faculty from those days remember rushing out to Fulton Street to catch a bus or ride a bicycle downtown as fast as they could so as not to be late to their next class. For a while, students were taxied back and forth in a black and white bus they jokingly called "the Black Mariah," slang for a police transport vehicle. The late 1940s saw a consolidation of the gains the college had made, and piece-by-piece the new campus came together with

The new campus was dedicated November 6, 1945, with Bishop Francis J. Haas presiding. President Bukowski is second priest from the right.

Father Bukowski became a monsignor in 1948. Here he greets students Geraldine Potts and Florence Wattson in front of Holmdene, the main campus building until 1955.

The Marian Congress annually drew thousands of the devout to Aquinas's campus in the late 1940s and 1950s.

new traditions. In May 1947, the first Marian Congress was held, an annual event thereafter that regularly drew thousands of people to the Robinson Road campus. The presence of so many GI Bill veterans had a decided effect on campus life inside and outside the classroom. Rodger Remington, longtime Aquinas history professor, was a seventeen-year-old freshman in 1947, and he remembers a group of thirty-eight veterans who lived near each other on Sigsbee Street near the Robinson Road campus. Each morning they would march, military style, to campus under the leadership of Colonel Bob McDonough. According to Remington, the vets would yank sleeping freshmen out of bed if they were not up and ready to march to their eight a.m. classes. In those days, students had to take eighteen hours of philosophy as part of their general education requirements, and the men who had seen the war firsthand brought difficult real-life examples to their ethics classes with Father Fay. The arguments and issues were not theoretical to them, and oftentimes class arguments would continue after class time was over.

Gradually, college life at Aquinas came to resemble postwar college life elsewhere. The first yearbook,

The Our Lady of Fatima shrine was built by returned student veterans in honor of the members of the Aquinas College community who died in World War II. It was dedicated in May 1950 and became the focal point of the Marian Congress each year.

The annual rite of the May crowning of the statue of the Blessed Virgin was long a part of college tradition. Here Dorothy Zeelbeck has the honor on May 6, 1950.

Thomist, was published in 1946. Students played volleyball on the lawn in front of Holmdene manor, sat on top of the lions to pose for pictures, and committed such college hi-jinks as one night removing all the toilet seats from the Holmdene bathrooms and hanging them on the trees outside. The first honors societies—Delta Epsilon Sigma and Kappa Gamma Pi—were started in 1950, and the college settled into the comfortable routine of the college calendar. Every October, a rosary procession was held. Between semesters, all Catholic students were expected to attend a three-day religious retreat. On March 7 each year, the college celebrated Academic Day when students and faculty processed around campus in academic regalia, went to a Solemn High Mass and honored outstanding students. One year, a medieval-style academic disputation was put on by four students on the "Foundation of Freedom of the

A mixer was held in Holmdene's library in 1945.

The first postwar prom was held at Blythefield Country Club in 1948.

Will." Towards the end of the academic year, there was the annual May crowning of Mary's statue. The Aquinas Circle, a monthly social gathering started in 1946, continued to sponsor dances, song fests, and socials. The junior-senior prom, which had fallen by the wayside during the war, was revived, often taking place at a suburban country club now rather than in a downtown hotel.[12]

Thomist was first published in 1946 and continued as the college yearbook until the 1970s.

The first athletic banquet was held in 1950 at the Eastern Avenue Hall where Athletic Director Joe Nagle awarded letters to forty-seven athletes who had competed the previous year. In the 1950s cheerleading was added as the college's first women's sports activity. Lloyd Brown thrilled Tommies fans as one of the premier basketball and track stars in the state, averaging 19.5 points per game and once scoring a college record of seventy-two. He led the team to its first ever victory over rival Calvin College in 1954.

By the mid-1950s, as the college continued to grow, Aquinas was again feeling the pinch of too little space. The library had outgrown its location on the old campus, with reports that librarians could not purchase new books because of lack of open shelf space. In addition, such new fangled technology as films, filmstrips, and classroom phonographs had to be housed as well. On the Robinson Road campus, Holmdene was serving as classroom, administration building, lunchroom, bookstore, the Women's League, the Men's Union, and residence for Monsignor Bukowski.[13] Classes were held in what were formerly the family's large bedrooms, some of which were still connected to old bathrooms with claw-footed tubs. The outbuildings like the Carriage House and the former stables were

Students check the posted schedule of upcoming classes in the early 1950s.

overflowing with students. As Bukowski noted in a mid-1950s annual report, the college was fifteen times larger than it had been back in 1922 when Sacred Heart College opened its doors. There were now forty-eight full-time faculty members. Growth is a good problem to have, but it is a problem nonetheless. It was clear by the early 1950's that the time had come for Aquinas to expand into its relatively new campus. And so, under the leadership of the Grand Rapids Dominicans, the college took yet another leap forward and launched an unprecedented ten-year building campaign.

Don Hampstead and John Criner played Algernon and Jack.

Student activities in the late 1940s and 1950s included Glee Club directed by Tony Brink. These singers pose in the stairwell of Holmdene in 1952.

Student theatrical productions were held off campus. This 1962 production of *The Importance of Being Earnest* was held at the Civic Theater downtown, with Ann Matesich and Sandra Earl as Gwendolyn and Cecily.

The 1953 basketball team with Coach and Athletic Director Joe Baker. The legendary Lloyd Brown, basketball and track standout, is second from right in the back.

Father B. Urban Fay coached the golf team in the 1940s..Here, the 1946 Tommies.

Members of the Spanish Club listen to the advantages of a summer trip to Cuba in 1948.

Tommy basketball player Dan Schmidt lays one up against Hillsdale in 1948. Aquinas College athletes were known as "The Tommies" until the mid-1970s.

Preengineering drafting classes were held in the upper level of the Carriage House.

An all-male class studies math with Robert Rosenbach and John Bellardo (in rear).

Endnotes

1. Sister Mona Schwind, *Period Pieces*, 241.
2. *Historically Speaking*, disc 1.
3. *Historically Speaking*, disc 1.
4. *Historically Speaking*, disc 1.
5. Schwind, 237.
6. Ibid.
7. Schwind, 240.
8. *Historically Speaking*, disc 1.
9. Schwind 244, and *Historically Speaking*, disc 1.
10. *Historically Speaking*, disc 1.
11. Bukowski, President's Report, 1947–48, 3.
12. *Historically Speaking*, disc 2.
13. Father Bukowski was elevated to the rank of monsignor in 1948.

Students in a crowded 1949 classroom study the Roman historian Livy and dream of a new academic building that will come in 1955.

Chapter 4

Building for the Future 1955–1968

At their 1948 Chapter, the Dominican sisters had voted to form a committee to study how they might consolidate the college's two campuses and provide for a new classroom and administration building. However, they did not make much progress until the Grand Rapids Fire Department, in 1951, raised issues concerning the old buildings on Ransom Street downtown. The nineteenth-century structures needed expensive renovation to bring them up to twentieth-century fire code.

Rather than incur the costs, the sisters decided to sell the property at 69 Ransom to the nearby YMCA for \$210,000.[1] By terms of the sale, the college had only eighteen months to move out, and in that time they would somehow have to provide for new science labs and music studios on the Robinson Road campus and find living space for the sisters and students who until then had resided downtown. The clock began to tick.

By May 1953, all the pieces seemed to be in place. A site for the new facility on the Robinson Road campus had been determined and plans were drawn-up by the architectural firm of D. A. Bohlen and Son of Indianapolis. A New York fundraising firm was contracted for a capital campaign, and Bishop Haas wrote to all the clergy of the Grand Rapids Diocese with a special appeal. In his letter, Haas stressed the special relationship that existed between the college and the parishes and schools of the diocese. He asked Catholics in the diocese to contribute to the campaign, noting that the sisters who graduated from Aquinas staffed many of their parish schools.

To make his point even more strongly, the bishop became the first donor for the new building, to the tune of \$5,000. Sadly, Bishop Haas died a few months after the campaign began and, like many other diocesan projects, the campaign ground to a halt. The spring after Bishop Haas's death, Pope Pius XII named Detroit Auxiliary Bishop Allen J. Babcock as the new leader of the Grand Rapids Diocese. Even though Aquinas College was the first stop on the new bishop's ceremonial motorcade into Grand Rapids, however, additional financial help would not come from the diocese for

The Administration Building tower became a symbol of Aquinas College.

The architect's original plans for the Administration Building called for separate wings for a chapel and library.

several years. Faced with the looming deadline for the turnover of the downtown property, the Dominican congregation took a second mortgage on its other properties and negotiated a $1.5 million loan from Northwestern Mutual Life Insurance Company to finance the new building.[2] Grand Rapids building firm Owen-Ames-Kimble was contracted to build the structure, and ground was broken on November 19, 1953. The entire college turned out in a formal academic procession, and, with Monsignor Bukowski and Mother Victor Flannery and several other sisters wielding shovels and picks, construction got underway. It was the first of many important groundbreakings that would take place in the next ten years.

A moment of prayer before the first major groundbreaking on campus, for the Administration (now Academic) Building.

Mother Victor Flannery was prioress of the Grand Rapids Dominicans during the years of the Aquinas College building boom.

The architects originally designed the Administration Building (as it was to be called) to have a large E-shaped footprint. The long front-façade would face the woodlot in the center of the campus, and the three extending wings would house a chapel, classrooms, and a library. The plan called for the building to be completed in several phases, but, as it turned out, the north and south wings (chapel and library) never materialized. (An architect's rendering of the original E-shaped plan can be found in the inside covers of the 1954 *Thomist*.)

The basement and foundation complete, the building's cornerstone was laid on a rainy day in late September 1954, with Bishop Babcock, the Board of Trustees, the Lay Advisory Board, faculty, students, and guests in attendance. Construction on the upper floors continued, with a deadline of the following summer.

Groundbreakings became familiar sights on Aquinas's campus in the 1950s and 1960s. The first was for the Administration (now Academic) Building, November 18, 1953. T. Gerald McShane, chair of the Lay Advisory Board, wields the shovel as Monsignor Bukowski (second from left), Mother Victor Flannery, and other dignitaries watch.

The 1954 construction of the Administration (later called Academic) Building allowed for vastly expanded classroom space and the closing of the downtown campus. Students David Bockheim, Elaine Randall, and John Ronan check out the materials as the building takes shape in the background.

In June 1955, the property at 69 Ransom was vacated and turned over to the YMCA. The Music Department's pianos and the biology and chemistry lab equipment were trucked up the hill to the new building, and summer classes inaugurated the Administration Building's use as a classroom. At the beginning of the regular academic year, students who had up until then had classes only in cramped Holmdene or in the ancient buildings downtown, marveled at their spacious new facility. In September, the administrative offices moved from Holmdene to the new building, and on October 11, the building was officially blessed and dedicated by Bishop Babcock. The cornerstone at the main entrance has the dates 1922–1955 carved on it, reminding all who passed that it had been thirty-three years since the founding of Sacred Heart College, when the first lay students were admitted. (After the opening of the Administration Building in 1955, the old Holmdene mansion, which had been the main building of the campus, became a residence for the teaching sisters until extensive renovations in the early 1980s converted it back to administrative and office space.)

The opening of the new building was only the beginning of the great wave of construction that would take place over the next ten years. In his annual report for 1956–57, Monsignor Bukowski reflected: "The amount of good done by the college in the intellectual, moral, and religious spheres is not calculable, but it is recorded in the archives of heaven. The solid hope is that the future will offer still more opportunity for service to the Church and to the country."[3]

Bricks and Mortar

The pace of growth began to increase for Aquinas in the late 1950s and early 1960s. The general economy was booming, and colleges and universities everywhere began to anticipate how they would accommodate the approaching tidal wave of Baby Boomers who were heading into their college years. The expanded academic facilities allowed the college to grow. Within three years, Aquinas's enrollment neared nine hundred, and the Dominicans, under the leadership of Mother Victor Flannery, asked their New York–based fundraising consultants to study the feasibility of expanding the physical plant further.

Three women students pose in front of the Administration Building in winter 1959.

Under the dynamic leadership of Mother Victor, and with the approval and support of Bishop Babcock, an ambitious fundraising campaign was undertaken. The fundraising consultants, Community Counseling Service of New York City, agreed to help raise $1.75 to $2 million for the project (later scaled down to $1.2 million). The goal was to build a science building, a residence for sisters in training, a new dormitory for women, and a physical education and assembly building in the next ten to twelve years.[4] The New York consultants would be aided by a committee of west Michigan business leaders, chaired by Peter M. Wege. With the sisters themselves doing much of the direct solicitation of funds, $1.3 million was raised by October 1959. The college hired Eugene Kennedy in that year to be its first-ever director of development, and a long-range fundraising goal of $8 million was set to lay a firm foundation for the college's future.[5]

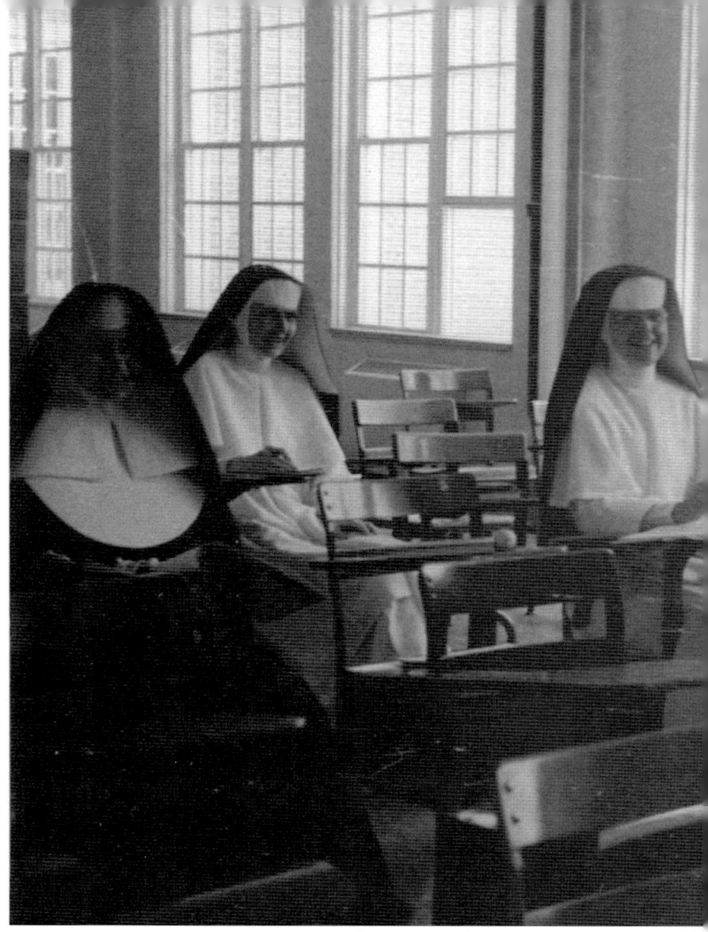

As the college became larger and more complex, it had to professionalize and, eventually, separate organizationally from the many other ministries and activities of the Dominican sisters of Grand Rapids. Congregational officials would remain as the college's official Board of Trustees for more than another decade, but a transition was begun. The college had had an Advisory Board composed of area laymen since 1942, but in the late 1950s that was expanded to a Lay Board of Trustees under C. Arthur Woodhouse and Joseph M. Walsh. With that move, responsibility for the college's budget management, long-range expansion and development slowly began to shift. The Dominican congregation continued until 1974 as the legal board and provided essential financial support

Dominican and other sisters made up the bulk of the student body in summer courses. Teaching at parochial schools during the academic year, they completed their degree requirements in summer sessions.

Peter Wege, longtime benefactor to the college, took leave from Steelcase Corporation to help raise funds for the college's 1960s building boom.

for the payment of mortgages. The fiscal safety net the Dominicans provided when the school faced financial emergencies remained vital to the college in those years. The college was taking its first steps toward being autonomous, and the close cooperation of the Marywood leadership, the Lay Board, and the college's administration and development office was essential.

Within the college, major shifts in the organizational structure were also needed. In the early days, faculty often served as part-time administrators, but those duties (e.g., deans of women and men, head of campus security) needed to become full-time administrative jobs. Additionally, as the college's debt increased during the building years, Monsignor Bukowski saw the need to rely increasingly on the business acumen of the Lay Board of Trustees. The growth spurt of the college's adolescence was on, but administering it was becoming unwieldy.[6]

The pace of the building boom was amazing. In 1957–58, Diehl and Diehl Architects were hired to formulate a campus master plan. In September 1959, ground was broken on the Robinson Road side of campus for the new three-story science building that would become Albertus Hall. In March 1960, ground was broken on Fulton Street for the House of Studies (now Hruby Hall), a residence for Dominican scholastics. In May of the same year, the college purchased the Gatehouse on Robinson Road which had once been part of the Lowe family estate but which was not included in the 1945 purchase of the property. The Gatehouse was used, first, as a residence for women students and later as the headquarters of the Development Department. In fall 1960, the new Albertus Hall was opened in a ceremony conducted by Bishop Babcock, and the old Albertus Hall, located in the Lowe carriage house, was briefly renamed Jarrett

Biology instructor Eugene Smith takes advantage of the campus's wide variety of trees to take a class outdoors.

A 1956 art class paints outdoors on the beautifully wooded and not yet heavily built campus.

The Class of 1960 plants a stake in the campus's future.

Hall before becoming The Carriage House in the late 1960s when it was converted into a theater. The completed House of Studies was dedicated by Bishop Babcock in June 1961, and over fifty sisters moved into it in November. Next, the cornerstone was laid for phase one of the new women's residence hall, to be known as Regina Hall, in September 1961. Regina Hall accepted its first students in September 1962. By the following year, more space for resident students was needed, and the college purchased the stately home known as Willowbrook for use as a women's residence. To accommodate increased numbers of resident male students, ground was broken in August 1963 for St. Joseph the Worker Hall, which was opened to students in 1964. Housing 156 male students and four counselors, St. Joe was located on the far western edge of campus, adjacent to Wilcox Park and St. Thomas the Apostle Parish. A combination tennis court and parking lot was built across the creek from St. Joe's.

Booming enrollment meant the school needed a proper student center to serve the needs of residents, and so in September 1965, the cornerstone was laid for Wege Center, which was to open in January 1966. Meanwhile, enrollment forced an expansion of Regina Hall. A new wing was added in 1967. The remaining major building project of the boom years was the construction of the Physical Education Building, for which ground was broken in December 1967. It opened in 1969.

The college's vigorous expansion was, in many ways, typical of the heady days of the late 1950s and early 1960s. American prosperity, the growing middle classes, and the first wave of Baby Boomers gave every indication that ongoing growth would continue forever. Change was in the wind, however. The Second Vatican Council, the Civil Rights movement, the 1963 assassination of John Kennedy, and the beginnings of military involvement in Vietnam were on the radar, but for the moment, life was good for Aquinas College.

In 1950, it had 971 full- and part-time students. By the 1960s, enrollment generally stood around 1,796, with 994 of those being full-timers. Tuition had increased from $120 to $220 per semester, and the faculty had grown to eighty-two, of whom twenty-six were sisters. A business administration major had been added in the early 1950s, and golf, track, and cross-country had been added to basketball and baseball as intercollegiate sports. Secretarial courses had disappeared, as had a short-lived Airline Stewardess Program. The college offered twenty-two major and minor subject areas. Aquinas College was reaching its maturity in good form.

Inside the New Buildings

The new Administration Building and Albertus Hall became the hallowed halls where academic pursuits were undertaken while the new residence halls became the scenes of student life—and nightlife. In the classrooms, longtime beloved (and sometimes feared) faculty held sway. The psychology courses of George LaMountain, the science courses of John "Doc" Poje, Dick McCormick, and Eugene Smith, and the literature courses of Frederick Bernard, Sister Marybride Ryan, and Sister Maris Stella Milhaupt shaped a future generation of therapists, physicians, writers, and teachers. Sister Malachi Laithwaite, librarian, built an outstanding children's literature collection from books purchased here and in England from personal acquaintances like Beatrix Potter and J. R. R. Tolkien and from antiquarian bookshops. Ralph Bennett, who joined the faculty in 1960, became legendary for his late hours—students could call until one a.m.—and for sometimes arriving to class in his Air Force Reserve uniform, straight from maneuvers. Sister Edward Mary taught students to think philosophically, and Dr. Jose Soler, a Renaissance man, taught Spanish.

Charles Frydrych, who came to Aquinas from Grand Rapids Catholic Central High School in 1959, and later became a physics professor at the college, recalls:

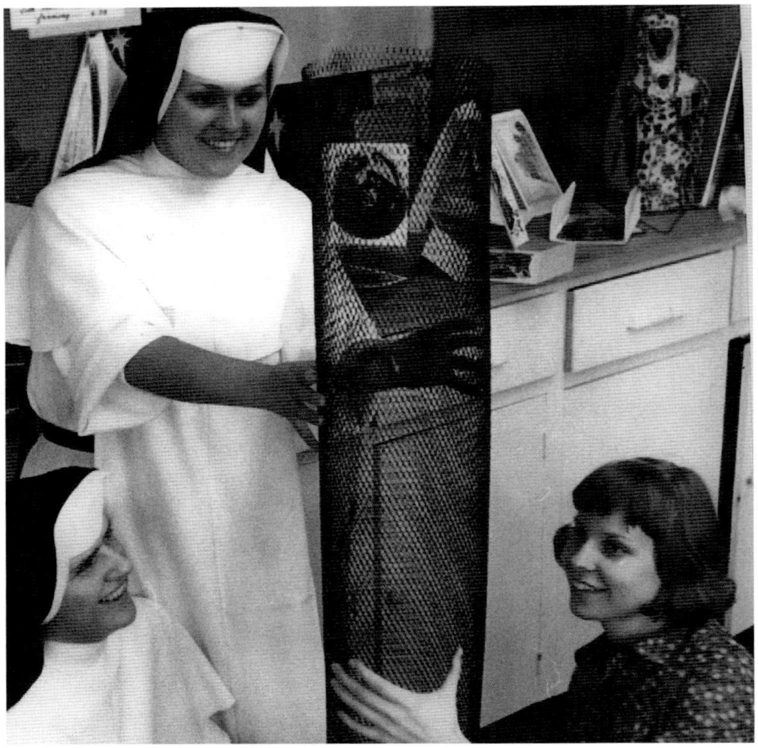

Sister Mary Yvonne and Carol Sakocius work on armatures for statues of the Nativity Scene in December 1963.

Dr. John Poje explained the intricacies of chemistry to generations of students.

When I came to Aquinas, there was this same kind of intellectual spirit that I saw in high school among the Dominican sisters. I was amazed that each course was taught by someone with this incredible background and focus. I had a marvelous freshman year, with Gert Horgan and Sister Ryan for English, Peter Erhardt in chemistry, all committed, sophisticated faculty. I was bowled over by this community of very bright and interesting people.[7]

In 1960, a language lab was built on the third floor of the Administration Building. Under the direction of Dr. Werner Prange, forty-two private acoustic-walled booths with recording and playback equipment drilled students in French, Spanish, German, and, for a short period, Swahili. With filmstrips, overhead projectors, and closed-circuit TV in the classrooms, Aquinas was a college at the technological cutting edge of the Space Age. Sister Mary de Chantal Luke, of the Theater Department, directed programs over WOOD-TV as an early experiment in distance learning. Other faculty appeared on WOOD-TV in two series, *Politics 1960* and *Ten O'Clock Scholar*. The college also inaugurated graduate degrees in theology, history, and English between 1960 and 1967. (These were later abandoned due to North Central's determination that they could not be supported by the college's small library.)

The enthusiasm for modern technology included a foray into closed-circuit television in the classroom. A 1961 self-study by the collegewide Planning Committee speaks rapturously of the possibilities of television in the classroom, in the same way that two decades later the next technology wave—the personal computer and the Internet—would excite another generation, but in the end the experiment led to little real change in the way classes were conducted.[8]

Student Life

Outside the classroom, the opening of the residence halls marked a big change in the culture of the college. Until then, female students were housed in buildings on Lake Drive that the college purchased or leased for the purpose but Lourdes, Siena, and Corby Halls, as they were called, could only accommodate a limited number of women students. Meanwhile, male students had to find apartments or houses to rent in Eastown or elsewhere. With the addition of the residence halls, however, all that changed, and a true campus life evolved. For the first time, the college also had the new problem of having hundreds of eighteen-to-twenty-year-old students on campus twenty-four hours a day.

Students staged a fundraiser in 1963 for a service trip to Bogota, Colombia, led by English professor Gertrude Horgan (not pictured).

In the late 1950s and early 1960s, colleges still served *in loco parentis* (in the place of parents), and rules were tight. It was not accidental that the men's hall, St. Joseph the Worker, had been built as far across campus as possible from the women's residence. Both halls had strict check-in times at night, those for the men one hour later than those for the women, on the presumption that the young gentlemen would see the young ladies home to Regina or Willowbrook before they themselves returned to their hall. Curfew was nine p.m. for women on weekdays and eleven p.m. on weekends. Quiet hours in the dorms were from seven p.m. until seven a.m., and all women had to wear skirts, with slacks allowed only for sports or recreation. Wednesday night was dress-up night, with men in suits and women in dresses, and Saturday night was steak night in the new Wege Center Cafeteria. No men were allowed in women's residence halls and vice versa, and only brief embraces were allowed as public displays of affection.

Wege Center gave students an on-campus venue for entertainment and recreation. In his annual report of 1965–66, Monsignor Bukowski noted that, "Wege Center, practically from the day it opened, became a student center in truth, with hardly a week or weekend going by without some student club or organization sponsoring an activity." Concerts, plays, Gala Weekend, the annual Carousel of Arts, and lectures by visiting scholars filled the building regularly.

Sometimes, of course, students needed to get off campus, and in those days the long arm of *in loco parentis* sometimes went after them. Freshman students were often surprised to find that one of the favorite hangouts of Aquinas students was called The Yacht Club. They couldn't figure out how there could be a boat club in the middle of the city or why students would go there in the winter; then they discovered that The Yacht Club in question was a bar on Wealthy Street in nearby Eastown. The club was a well-attended watering hole on the weekends, but the college kept watch. Longtime faculty member Betty Jennings recalled that one of her first jobs as assistant to Dean of Women Gertrude Horgan was to sit with her in a car parked outside the Yacht Club, using the

The Aquinas College Chorus, 1964.

Chris Longcore gets into the spirit of Gala Weekend by purchasing a hat from the Dominican Sisters' hat booth.

most recent yearbook to ID students going in and out. According to Jennings, Dean Horgan even had informants working inside the bar. "She ignored state rules [about drinking ages]," Jennings recalled, "Her rules were a higher law."[9]

Of course, Horgan was more than a disciplinarian. Alumni of the early 1970s remember her as one of the shapers of the Ireland Program, and she also organized Operation Latin America, in which students worked in Bogota, Colombia, for three months in the summer of 1963. They had raised $4,000 to go work with the poor in the city, and the following winter nineteen Colombian students came to Aquinas for two months. Such service was integral to the college's mission. That same summer, Monsignor Bukowski led a group of thirteen students to Guatemala where they spent eleven weeks teaching, constructing, doing social and clinical work.[10] Bukowski also led service trips to Appalachia during this period. Concern with social justice issues flourished on campus as the Civil Rights

Gala Weekend from the 1960s until the 1980s often had an Oktoberfest theme.

The 1957 Gala Weekend as pictured in *Thomist*.

Richard Seymour, Bette Tarte, Fran Novak, and Dr. Francis A. Rosamond check out bookstore offerings in the early 1960s.

Students continue the college tradition of the Aquinas Circle, a monthly social gathering, in 1963.

The *Thomist* yearbook was a feature of college life in the 1950s.

Sister Angus Black, O.P., fed generations of Aquinas students in her well-supervised kitchen.

The cast of *The Bells Are Ringing* (1967) included future judge Dennis Lieber (in fedora, center).

The Carriage House theater provided an intimate venue for productions such as 1967's *Under Milk Wood*, with faculty member Herb Martin (seated) and (left to right) Jim Milanowski, William Schultz, Roberta Zimber, and Theresa Grywalski.

Jim Chervenka and Jessica Starr played multiple roles in 1967's *Under Milk Wood*

Under Milk Wood program.

The Aquinas Award was given annually to luminaries in the world of the arts, service, and intellectual life.

movement gathered steam in America. One alumnus even recalls an Aquinas boycott of The Yacht Club when the club refused to serve a student who was a member of a minority.

The service ethic was articulated by Monsignor Bukowski this way in 1966:

It was said not too many years ago that colleges and universities are the "thinking part" of society. Today, however, the concept of the role of educational institutions has greatly broadened to include, in addition to the thinking part of society, a great deal of action—of providing many types of community service.

The college provides graduates equipped not only to give intellectual leadership but also to serve their communities in teaching, social work, business, and various professions.... [The college] must be a tireless critic of mediocrity and complacency, an uncompromising herald of new challenges. One of its functions is to be in the vanguard of human advancement.[11]

Saints basketball standout Dennis Alexander goes up for the ball. He became the first Aquinas player to score over two thousand points in his collegiate career.

John Kurzynowski became NCAA small college national champion golfer in 1964. Kurzynowski was part of Aqinas's nationally ranked golf teams in the early 1960s.

Coach Bob Sullivan led the Tommies' baseball squads to victory in the 1950s.

Cheerleading became the first women's sport activity in the mid-1950s.

The Physical Education and Assembly Building opened in 1969. In the opening game, the Aquinas Tommies defeated longtime rival Calvin College.

Extracurricular activities flourished at Aquinas in the 1960s. Even in the absence of a theater building, Sister Mary de Chantal and Jack Rang brought forth memorable student productions of plays like *The Importance of Being Earnest* (1962), *Cyrano de Bergerac* (1963), *Arms and the Man* (1963), and *A Man for All Seasons* (1964). In 1966, the Carriage House was renovated into a small theater that brought an intimate performance space to campus for such well-remembered theater-in-the-round productions as Dylan Thomas's *Under Milk Wood*, with faculty member Herbert Martin starring among the student performers.

A 1960s film series that featured then avant-garde films by Ingmar Bergman and Federico Fellini gained some notoriety in the city when it screened Bergman's *Virgin Spring* (1960) that features a brutal rape scene in the middle of the film. A controversy erupted over the appropriateness of such a film being shown on a Catholic college campus, and English professor Frederick Bernard published a masterful defense and demonstration of the difference between art and pornography.

Student activities included the regular publication of the *Aquinas Herald* and occasional appearances of a mysterious alternate newsletter known as *The Phantom* that appeared erratically until school authorities almost, but not quite, figured out who was responsible for it. Sister Marybride Ryan led a new literary publication, with the space-age title *The Orbit* that featured student poetry and fiction. Students presented an annual Carousel of Arts for several years in the spring, and, in 1962, Father Hugh Michael Beahan began broadcasting classical music and news of interest to Catholics from the tower of the Administration Building on WXTO Radio, providing students with media training.

The annual Aquinas Award was begun in 1959, with the first recipient being Grand Rapids businessman and Serra International president J. Bernard Haviland. The Aquinas Award subsequently was given to such luminaries as *Saturday Review* editor Norman Cousins, and Madonna House director Baroness Catherine de Hueck, theater luminaries Alfred Lunt and Lynn Fontanne, as well as to Joseph Foust, an Aquinas alumnus who performed unpaid medical service and built a hospital in Tanganyika.[12]

Sports continued to play a prominent role in college life, with the 1961 baseball and golf teams winning city championships, and the cross-country team compiling a 35-5 record over several years. Basketball star Denny Alexander scored a career total of 2,034 points in those years, and John Kurzynowski won the NCAA college division national championship in golf in 1964. The outstanding golf teams of that era earned the Tommies the nickname the "Yankees of the North" among Southern teams at national meets. During this time, Aquinas joined the National Association of Intercollegeiate Athletics (NAIA) after it and the NCAA ruled that schools had to declare affiliation to one conference or another. Crowning the decade in sports, the athletic program finally got what it had desired for years when the last important building of the boom years was opened in 1969, the Physical Education and Assembly Building, known by all simply as the Fieldhouse. At the opening basketball game, the Tommies defeated the Calvin College Knights to inaugurate the new facility. For the first time, the Aquinas indoor sports programs had a permanent home.

Monsignor Bukowski receives Lear Siegler Inc.'s gift of an analog computer in spring 1968. As Monsignor Bukowski prepared to retire, the world of education was about to change forever.

"Mon Buk!"

On January 29, 1968, Monsignor Arthur Bukowski announced that he would retire from the school that he had guided through three decades of monumental change. Under his leadership, the college had grown from a small Catholic junior college downtown to a respected four-year liberal arts college on a modern multifacility campus. His priestly presence through three decades of leadership endeared him to many students. On January 29, 1969, his last day as president, Aquinas College's only student uprising took place. A fairly large contingent of students marched towards the main entrance of the Administration Building bearing placards. But this was no protest march. The marchers joyfully rushed into the president's office, hustled him outside into the back seat of a waiting convertible, and proceeded to parade him around campus chanting their affectionate nickname for him, "Mon Buk!" Some student placards read "Buk for Pope!" The event was mentioned later by commentator Paul Harvey on his nationally syndicated radio program as an example of a student anti-protest march.

The monsignor's optimism never wavered. In the mid-1960s, speaking of himself in the third person, he wrote:

The president is increasingly conscious of the magnitude of the task involved in providing higher education under Catholic auspices. He does not, however, share the pessimistic outlook of those who predict the demise of the independent college. He has faith in the education value of such institutions, in the ability of the American people to recognize these values as well as in their willingness to preserve them, and above all in the Divine Providence upon whose help and guidance all must ultimately depend.[13]

Though he was leaving Aquinas, his career was far from over. He spent a year in Appalachia as a missionary, then returned to Grand Rapids and served as a priest for the Grand Rapids Diocese, teaching at St. Joseph Seminary. When ill health forced him to move to St. Ann's Home, he continued to serve, saying Mass for the residents until in the end he became too weak to stand. Monsignor Arthur Bukowski died on October 10, 1989, and his funeral Mass, concelebrated by the bishop and many of the city's priests, filled St. Andrew's Cathedral. His retirement and passing marked the end of an era. In 1989, the college's pastoral center was named after him.

Endnotes

1. Sister Mona Schwind, *Period Pieces*, 262.
2. Schwind, 263.
3. Bukowski, 1956–57 Annual Report, 2.
4. Schwind, 265.
5. Ibid.
6. Bukowski, President's Report, 1964–65.
7. *Historically Speaking*, disc 3.
8. "Aquinas College Final Report of College Planning Committee," June 30, 1961, 34–35.
9. *Historically Speaking*, disc 3.
10. President's Report, 1963–64, 8.
11. President's Report, 1966.
12. Ibid.
13. President's Report, 1965–66, 1.

SUM-
MA
THEOLO
GICA
NOTHING
but

Chapter 5

The Future Arrives 1969–1986

The college that greeted Aquinas College's second president, Dr. Norbert Hruby in 1969 was essentially the same college it had always been. The student body was 95 percent Catholic, 96 percent eighteen to twenty-two years old, composed of middle and lower middle class men and women in about equal numbers. Most of them were the first generation in their German, Irish, or Polish families to attend college. Liberal arts graduates led the pack, making up 86 percent of the graduates, with business graduates making up the remaining 14 percent.

Self-Study

Through the 1950s, the majority of the faculty had been religious sisters and priests, but by the late 1960s, the ratio was beginning to shift, and in 1969 nearly two-thirds of the faculty were lay people. However, 75 to 80 percent of these lay faculty were Catholic.[1] In other words, there were few signs of the monumental shifts that were about to shake Aquinas and the country and leave a significantly changed institution by the time Hruby retired seventeen years later.

Hruby came to Aquinas with a rich background. He had been a director of the Public Information Center at Loyola University in Chicago in the early 1950s, then moved to the University of Chicago, where he eventually became associate dean. From there, he moved to Mundelein College outside Chicago, where he served as vice president. At Mundelein he acquired the skills and background that made him the right choice to succeed Monsignor Bukowski. While there, he had undertaken a thorough self-study that took the college into new and mostly uncharted educational territory. Sensing there was a latent desire for higher education among people who ordinarily would not think of themselves as "college students," Hruby began a degree completion program at Mundelein that targeted mature women who may have never gone to college or who interrupted their college careers to raise their families in the 1950s. The program was a great success.

By the time Hruby applied for the job of president of Aquinas College, most people realized the college

The seven-hundredth anniversary of Thomas Aquinas's death brought famed theologian Bernard Lonergan, S.J., and other notables to campus throughout the year in 1974.

had some catching up to do if it was to survive in the new educational climate of the late 1960s. The rise of community colleges changed the landscape of who

Dr. Norbert Hruby guided the college through massive change in the turbulent period between 1969 and 1986.

went to college and where they went, and locally a new state institution, Grand Valley State Colleges, was born to the west of Grand Rapids and already threatened to siphon off students. There was generally great ferment nationwide on college campuses as the tumultuous decade known now as "The Sixties" continued to unfold. Campus takeovers by student radicals, the overturning of traditional curricula, antiwar protests, the effect of the assassinations of John Kennedy, his brother Robert, and Martin Luther King, Jr., as well as the urban unrest in Detroit and other cities spelled the end of quiet, traditional liberal arts education as it had been. As a Catholic college, Aquinas faced the additional challenge of understanding and implementing the reforms mandated by the Second Vatican Council in the early 1960s.

Hruby embraced the difficulties of the times, and rather than retrench the college and try to preserve it as it had been, he decided to take it into the future. He made it a prerequisite for his hire that he be allowed to begin a massive self-study of the college with the goal of preserving the best of what the college offered and then moving into the future with new policies and programs. He was not shy about his ambitions. In fact, he titled his inaugural address in May 1969, "Revolution at Aquinas."

Hruby began, "This is the day the Lord has made—not for me, but for this indomitable little private liberal arts college which does not realize it is an anachronism. It does not realize that some of the most serious students of higher education in America have decided that this kind of school is obsolescent if not quite obsolete. . . ."[2] He noted that in the age of the emerging multiversity small liberal arts colleges like Aquinas were in danger of becoming extinct. His view of the context was realistic, if somewhat grim, yet he did not believe that the college was fated to die. Instead, he called for another kind of revolution to remake Aquinas College from the inside out, without its losing its distinctiveness. "[W]e cannot set out with a comfortable baggage of ideas which we can fall back on in case the going gets thick. We start by trying to find out exactly who we are and what we are doing—good, bad, or indifferent." His process was inclusive, involving students, faculty, staff, and alumni, as well as a panel of nationally known higher education experts. "If Aquinas graduates of the future are to cope with that world, we have to make some radical changes in what happens to them while they are our students."[3]

This was not mere inauguration day rhetoric. Under the deputy directorship of professor Lee Jacokes, a massive, fifteen-month sequence of questionnaires, study groups, panels, committees, and subcommittees was already underway. Starting in February, various constituencies of the college had compiled lists of

Dr. Lee Jacokes guided the 1969–1970 Self-Study process that transformed the college.

questions they would like answered. Submitted on 3x5 index cards, the questions were mostly serious, sometimes frivolous, but always challenging. Lee Jacokes estimates that there were about five thousand questions submitted. After sifting through those questions, formal questionnaires were prepared to reflect the concerns of members of the college community.

In July 1969, a thirty-page questionnaire was sent to all Aquinas alumni requesting exhaustive data about their socio-economic status, education, and professional life, as well as opinions on a wide variety of subjects from politics to religion and education. Even such apparent trivia as respondents' favorite musicians and writers was solicited. The questionnaire even had a section for the spouses of alumni to fill out. That fall, current students were given a sixty-four-page questionnaire that sought their opinions on everything from curricular matters to living arrangements and meal preferences. In a cover letter to the students, Hruby wrote of the importance of this survey: "On it depends, in a very real sense, the ultimate effectiveness of our brave experiment in re-invention." The student portion of the self-study, he said, is "the single most important research tool and fact-and-opinion-finding device in the whole of the Self-Study." This serious solicitation of student participation was a sign of Hruby's intention to make the self-study inclusive. Administrators were given questionnaires more focused on their professional areas, and every faculty member was expected to be part of a study group or committee for the duration of the study.

Jacokes dealt with the everyday organizing and supervision of the Self-Study, including collating and coordinating the immense amount of information gathered and laboriously entering that information on IBM punch cards for computer processing. A Board of six nationally known education experts was convened three times during the process. The Board's job was to listen to the various subcommittees' progress reports and to give feedback and direction.

In Phase II of the Self-Study, the survey data was fed to study groups for discussion that eventually led to written reports. The main study groups were on governance, faculty rights and responsibilities, student rights and responsibilities, teaching resources and theory, and learning resources and theory. Each group of fifteen to twenty people included a mix of students, faculty, and staff. One instructor joked later that everyone was so busy with committee work that little classroom education took place, but in spite of the sometimes-tedious process, Jacokes and Hruby were able to keep the campus motivated to continue the conversation, even as critics of the process took pot shots at it.

A crucial part of the process was a series of visits to other campuses to observe how they were handling change and renovation at their institutions. The visits came about a full year into the Self-Study, a time of frustration and exhaustion when many were ready to give up on the process, doubting that anything meaningful would come of it. Tension grew until a showdown meeting was held between the administration and the disgruntled study groups. At that meeting, the groups were somehow convinced to continue the difficult Self-Study process and to proceed to the campus visitation stage. Jacokes recommended that Aquinas suspend all classes and close for a full week so that all the campus visitations could take place at once. The travel expenses were paid for by a grant from the Grand Rapids Foundation.

In the second week of March 1970, teams of five from the various study groups set off to observe twenty-eight colleges and universities in the Midwest, some small like Aquinas, others large. The groups spent three days at the other schools, usually with great access to administrators, students, and faculty, and they returned with fresh ideas and a renewed confidence that many of the things Aquinas was thinking of trying were far ahead of other institutions. Both Hruby and Jacokes credited these off-site visits with salvaging the Self-Study process and giving participants new energy to prepare for the upcoming visit of the Advisory Board.

The fifteen-month process came to a dramatic close on Saturday, May 6, 1970. The atmosphere of the meeting was supercharged not just because it was the culmination of fifteen months of work that had turned the campus inside out, but also because of events in the outside world that galvanized colleges across the United States. Two days before the meeting, the killings at Kent State had taken place; the week before the Cambodian incursion had escalated the war in Vietnam. As Hruby later wrote, "While the whole educational establishment seemed about to go up in flames, Aquinas College was having the most important faculty meeting in its history."[4]

The outcome of the meeting was up for grabs. Any changes in curriculum or governance would have to be approved by the Faculty Assembly, but enacting the study group recommendations would, in many cases, remove power from the Faculty Assembly and distribute it to a new bicameral assembly structure that gave students and administrators increased voice and power. If the faculty would not vote to reduce its own power, none of the changes proposed by the Self-Study would get enacted. The faculty, staff, and students discussed and debated for thirteen hours. By 10:03 p.m., when the meeting finally adjourned, they had basically created a new Aquinas College.

A New Aquinas College

The range of changes coming out of the Self-Study was astonishing. In addition to the new bicameral governance structure calling for a new constitution, a more flexible curriculum was established. In the spirit of the times, core requirements were reduced and students were given a wide menu of course options. Degree requirements were simplified. Academic disciplinary boundaries were adjusted or taken down. Flexible scheduling, a new grading scale, and opportunities for life experience credit, independent study, and off-campus study were increased. On the student life side, the old *in loco parentis* regulations were considerably relaxed, and student rights were given more attention.[5] In 1972, a residence hall was opened to co-ed housing for the first time. In short, at a time when other campuses were convulsed with violence, bombings, and protests, Aquinas College had pulled off a quiet revolution, entering the 1970s as a reinvented place. The changes were not without their critics. Professor George LaMountain—no surprise to those who knew him—issued a 117-page minority report criticizing the changes. But the grueling work of the Self-Study was accomplished. Now came the hard part: implementing the momentous changes and helping Aquinas survive during a time when hundreds of other small, private liberal arts colleges—"invisible colleges," as they were called—collapsed in the new academic and political environment.

Innovate, Innovate, Innovate!

Aquinas College made its formal institutional break from the Grand Rapids Dominicans in 1974. In a move that caused controversy within the Dominican community, a transition was made to a lay Board of Trustees. The prioress and other members of the Dominican leadership would continue to be ex-officio members of the college's Board, and many sisters would continue to teach and administer at the school, but the Dominican congregation was no longer liable for the college's periodic financial crises and shortfalls, or its loan obligations. The new Aquinas College was, in terms of the law anyway, "on its own."

With its new curriculum in place, and with institutional autonomy, Aquinas faced its next challenge. Simple demographics showed that the number of eighteen-year-olds was about to decline as the Baby Boomer bulge moved through higher education. At the same time, there was rising competition from schools that were larger, cheaper and, like Grand Valley State Colleges, destined to grow. If Aquinas was going to hold its own and even expand, it had to continue to offer a quality education to traditional undergraduates and, at the same time, find new markets for higher education. This would call for, "an acute sense of serendipity, a genuine relish for adventure, and a streak of courage."[6]

Using the market-research skills developed during the Self-Study, the college set about looking for potential pupils who didn't fit the early 1970s profile of "college students." In the ensuing years, this appeal to nontraditional students would become Aquinas's hallmark and financial salvation.

The Career Action Program (CAP)

One of the goals of Hruby's entrepreneurship was to keep the classrooms filled for as many hours as possible during the week. The Career Action Program was created for working men and women who wished to advance their careers by completing a college degree. Dr. R. J. Bennett had been pushing for such a program for years, and when asked to take on responsibility for developing the program early in 1969, he leapt at it with his usual energy and military discipline. Primarily business and career oriented, CAP courses were offered on Saturdays and weeknight evenings in an innovative format that met for twelve weeks once a week for four hours. By taking one class per week through the year, students could earn twelve credits per year towards their degrees. Bennett reached out to the local business community to bring in specialist teachers for career courses while relying on full-time faculty to teach the more theoretical parts of the curriculum. He tirelessly visited personnel directors

The Career Action Program brought adult learners to campus to improve their professional skills starting in 1969. They were typically working adults who wished to improve their job skills through earning a college degree.

The Encore Program allowed mature women to complete their college education at convenient hours.

In the 1970s, Aquinas's student body was made up of large numbers of adult learners.

at local businesses to describe the program and to leave brochures for the employees of local companies. Within two years, the program had recruited over five hundred students, and enrollment swelled to seven hundred a few years after that.

Encore!

In the late 1960s and early 1970s, only half of the women in America who had ever attended college actually completed their degrees. Following the dominant pattern of the 1950s and 1960s, these women left school and dreams of careers behind when they got married. By 1970, there was a backlog of women who might be eager for an opportunity to complete their college degrees. Aquinas responded with surprising flexibility to these students' special needs and was rewarded with a quickly growing new program called Encore, headed by English instructor Joan Crandall, a woman who could easily relate to the Encore students. (The program was taken over later by Jane Hibbard Idema.) Encore scheduled convenient class times and accepted credits from any college no matter when they were earned on the presumption that the women's maturity and life experience would more than make up for the length of time since they had last taken classes. The typical profile of an Encore student was of a woman in her early to mid-thirties with at least one child in school. In the first year of classes, the Encore students enrolled in special courses, but within a year they were mainstreamed into the regular courses of the college. One Encore student, a mother of three school-age children, said, "I had nothing definite in mind, except that I wanted an education, had waited a long time to have this opportunity. . . . The women, the classes, the situations that were introduced to me have opened up all kinds of doors, and I think I have utilized every class I've ever had here to one extent or another."[7]

In those Encore years, it became common at Aquinas College commencements to hear sporadic shouts of "Yay, Mom!" as graduates proudly strode across stage to receive their degrees.

Emeritus College

It occurred to the Continuing Education division that another group who might be interested in further education was the elderly. Director of Continuing Education R. Paul Nelson asked Dr. Carl Pettersch, retired dean of graduate studies at the University of Western Connecticut, to conduct a broad market survey of the elderly in Kent and Ottawa Counties. Supported by grants from the National Endowment for the Humanities and the Michigan Council for the Humanities, the study, called "Post-Retirement Feasibility Study," led to a pilot program that was launched with two seminar series, moderated by Aquinas faculty member Ken Marin, in the spring of 1975. Forty-eight retired people from various walks of life took both seven-session seminars. Pettersch called them "an atypical and unusually demanding group of students." The experience revealed that this group of students was interested not only in so-called retirement issues but also in the arts, humanities, current events, and sciences. The college realized these still active people wanted to turn this potentially dull time of their lives into "positive, creative, and beneficial use." The program, eventually called Emeritus College, sought to "enable senior citizens to cope with life and to lead fuller, richer, more meaningful lives."[8] In the fall of 1975, Emeritus offered three classes attended by 115 individuals, and from there the program quickly grew, becoming one of the very earliest senior continuing education programs in the country. (The first Emeritus courses predated the internationally known Elderhostel by one year.) The first director of the Emeritus College was Sister Agnes Thiel. The University of Michigan's Dr. Howard McCluskey, one of America's foremost experts on adult education and the educational needs of the elderly said "that the undertaking was unique in this country and well worth pursuing further."[9]

The Emeritus College was one of the first programs in the country to serve the educational needs of people fifty-five and older.

In its nearly forty-year history, the Emeritus College has continued to grow, offering courses year round. In 2008, after receiving a major grant from the Osher Foundation, the name of Emeritus was changed to the Osher Lifelong Learning Institute at Aquinas College (OLLI), but the Emeritus name lives on in the annual Aquinas Norbert J. Hruby Emeritus Award given to individuals who have excelled in service to the community throughout their lives.

Master of Management

The success of the Career Action Program led the college to explore the possibility of offering a graduate business degree. Business professor Norman Tychson, Paul Nelson, director of continuing education, and a small team went into the business community and asked what their needs were. All agreed that west Michigan did not need another MBA program emphasizing number crunching. Aquinas, with its liberal arts tradition and people-oriented approach, was in an ideal position to offer something different. The market for the master of management degree would be people in various professions who were in supervisory positions, or who wished to be. They had professional expertise in their fields but didn't need advanced accounting to move forward in their careers. Instead, they needed training in how to manage people, do strategic planning, and effectively motivate workers. Master of management courses were first

Professors Linda Easley, Thomas Edison, and Michael Williams (seated) and President Hruby and Sister James Rau, O.P., look over plans for the Eastown Community Association, which the college was instrumental in founding.

offered in 1977–78. Small class sizes, convenient course times, and flexible scheduling—the hallmarks of Aquinas at this time—made the program a success from the start. At one point, before other local colleges developed similar programs, five hundred students were enrolled.

Eastown!

By the late 1960s, early signs of urban decay were noticeable in the area around the Aquinas campus. The number of rental properties had increased, as had the number of low-income residents. The people who had lived in the area for a long time were aging, while new residents with households headed by persons under age twenty-five were increasing. Middle-class families headed by middle-aged parents were fleeing to the suburbs. Crimes like burglary, auto theft, and even arson were increasing and nearby Wilcox Park was getting a reputation as a punk hangout.

President Hruby realized that the future stability of the college depended on its being located in

The book *Eastown! A report on how Aquinas College helped its local community reverse neighborhood transition and deterioration* became a guidebook for many community organizing efforts nationally.

The first-ever Eastown Street Fair in 1973, became an annual neighborhood tradition at the corner of Wealthy Street and Lake Drive.

a stable neighborhood, so in the fall of 1971, he called together members of the college community to study how the college could work with the neighborhood. Under the leadership of professors Linda Easley, anthropologist; Thomas Edison, urban geographer; and Michael Williams, who had considerable community organization experience in Milwaukee prior to coming to Grand Rapids, the college neighborhood study committee spent a year meeting with local experts, statisticians from the City and County Health Departments, urban planners, and members of the Grand Rapids Board of Education.[10] Edison's urban geography class did an in-depth survey of the area now known as Eastown. The data showed that the situation was serious. Frank Fallon, executive director of the Greater Grand Rapids Housing Corporation, told the study group he saw little hope for the neighborhood unless the college got involved. "Aquinas must assist metropolitan movements as well as embark upon the crucial task of neighborhood organization."[11]

Mary Alice Williams at Eastown Community Hall in the 1970s. The organization received a grant from the Kellogg Foundation to pay the salaries of its community organizers.

On January 8, 1973, President Hruby invited one hundred residents of the surrounding community to campus and shared with them the results of the study group's work. Two weeks later, he invited merchants from the Wealthy–Lake Drive business district to campus and repeated the report. Out of these meetings came a steering committee of fourteen volunteers, block coordinators, and officers. They planned and pulled off the first successful Eastown Street Fair at the intersection of Lake Drive and Wealthy Street. Spirits boosted by that success, the newly named Eastown Community Association moved into an office on Wealthy Street that fall. The first director was John Fodor, an Aquinas alumnus. In January 1974, the organization got an infusion of cash in the form of a $129,836 grant from the W. K. Kellogg Foundation that enabled the ECA to pay its staff of two persons and maintain its office. The grant also provided funds for developing closer ties between the college and the organization and provided paid stipends for Aquinas faculty to work with the Community Association and to develop a relevant urban studies curriculum.

The banner of the Eastown Community Association became synonymous with urban action, and within a few years the neighborhood had changed and stabilized. Subsequently, the annual Eastown! Street Fair has become an institution and the neighborhood maintains its integrated, artsy, somewhat funky 1960s feel year round.

Controversy

In the volatile days of the early 1970s, Aquinas experienced one major convulsion that challenged its values. The graduating seniors of 1974, with the faculty and Board of Trustees' approval, invited Congresswoman Shirley Chisholm to be their commencement speaker. The Board voted her an honorary degree. Chisholm, representative of the Bedford-Stuyvesant area of New York City, was primarily known as an educator, author, and Civil Rights advocate, as well as being the first black woman to make a credible run for president of the United States in 1972. Lesser known was that she had written in support of *Roe v. Wade*. This became known to the college community one month before graduation and the campus erupted. Chisholm at one point offered to step aside, but after a tense three-hour meeting, the Board of Trustees reaffirmed the invitation. A deeply divided faculty voted roughly three-to-two to award the honorary degree. Letters to the editor flowed in daily, and Bishop Breitenbeck resigned his honorary trusteeship of the college. On graduation day, Representative Chisholm, in spite of bomb threats and picketing, addressed the graduates under very tight security. There was a standing ovation for her, but the wounds took a long time to heal.[12]

The Anglers' Rest is one of two pubs in the village of Tully Cross.

Students and faculty study by firelight in the intimacy of the cottages in Tully Cross.

Ireland Program

Aquinas's Ireland Program was first proposed in January 1972 by Gertrude Horgan, then a member of the English Department and dean of women. Horgan had a long love of Ireland and Irish culture and thought students other than language majors should have opportunity for foreign study. From the beginning, the intended curriculum included Irish literature, culture, and history, as well as a commitment to working with and in the local community. Various Aquinas instructors would be in charge of the program, receiving training in Irish literature and history, and teaching courses from their own disciplines adapted to the conditions in Ireland.

The Ireland semester has drawn Aquinas students and faculty to the village of Tully Cross, in Connemara, for forty years. The thatched cottages provide a cultural immersion experience for students every winter.

The program was given a trial run in Lewisburgh, Ireland, in academic year 1972–73, but while Horgan was in Ireland with the first group of students, she and her companion Ann Quinn happened to drive through the village of Tully Cross where they had the fortune to meet local publican Paddy Coyne. Coyne—who owned the pub and a local store and was also the town's funeral director—was one of the heads of the recently formed organization Connemara West that promoted tourism in the remote region. At the time, Connemara West was constructing nine traditional Irish thatched-

A toga party in the shadow of Tully Mountain.

roof cottages intended for summer tourist rentals. Thoroughly charmed by Coyne and the village, Horgan decided that henceforth the Aquinas Ireland Program would be located there. In 1974, the winter-spring program moved to the Renvyle Cottages in Tully Cross, a village so small that the twenty-five Aquinas students and two faculty members doubled its size.

Since the program was founded, generations of Coynes, Curleys, Sammons, and other local families have welcomed Aquinas students and faculty. Longtime friendships, and even a few marriages have resulted. Students and faculty treasure memories of the Easter morning climb up Tully Mountain, the side trips to the Isle of Inishbofin, the Giants' Causeway, and the dramatic Cliffs of Moher. They remember their dinner at Bunratty Castle, and their visit to the prehistoric site Newgrange. Early students remember the wild donkeys coming into town before donkey refuges were created in Connemara. Returning Ireland alums treasure a pint or two at Paddy Coyne's Pub or the other watering hole in town, The Angler's Rest, and they may stop into Christ the King Church for a prayer of thanks for the experience.

Though the weather can be severe on the west coast of Ireland in the months between January and May, Ireland alumni know that after every gale, when the howling wind stops blowing the rain sideways off the ocean, there come moments of unparalleled beauty when the sun and mist conspire to create the most beautiful rainbows in the world. One of the most commonly heard expressions on Aquinas College's campus in early May is, "I left my heart in Tully Cross!"

Aquinas College's Jazz Festival (1973–2003) brought up to twenty college jazz bands to campus annually to perform a weekend of non-stop jazz.

Aquinas College Jazz Festival (1973–2003)

In 1973, Dr. Bruce Early founded what was to become a long-lasting musical tradition at Aquinas, the Aquinas College Jazz Festival. During the first years, the program consisted of a weekend of jazz workshops and performances by six or seven college jazz bands, but by 1981, the number had grown to over twenty, which performed virtually nonstop jazz from Friday afternoon through Sunday. The festivals featured clinics with working musicians who had been side players and studio musicians with some of America's jazz greats. Well-known stars like George Benson (in 1997) and Vince Di Martino (in 1998) represented some of the big names who came, and Michigan jazz performers like Fred Keller (in 1999) and Edie Evans Hyde (in 2000) added their star quality to the weekend. As many as four hundred jazz-loving college musicians attended, mostly from Michigan and Indiana schools with strong music programs, and awards were given for outstanding student performers. In 1989, high school groups were added to the mix and the festival got bigger than ever.

Professional jazz musicians like Andy Goodrich gave workshops to college jazz musicians.

After Bruce Early's untimely death in 1998, the tradition continued under Dr. Paul Brewer and Music Department chair Barbara Witham-McCargar until 2003 when it was discontinued to allow the Music Department to develop its excellent summer jazz camps for high school students.

Dr. Bruce Early (lower right on trombone) was the driving force behind the annual Aquinas College Jazz Festival.

And More . . .

Energized by the spirit of the times, Aquinas became a hotbed of educational experimentation and entrepreneurship in the 1970s. In addition to the ongoing success of the programs already mentioned, the college developed many other initiatives, some of which had shorter lives than others. The IDEA Program, or Individually Designed Education for Adults, evolved out of Paul Nelson's Summer School Without Walls. Modeled on the low-residency programs of Goddard College in Vermont, IDEA offered individualized programs of study for adult students who wished to complete a degree.

To fill classrooms in the summer, the College Expectations Program (CEP) was aimed at high school juniors and seniors who were not sure whether they had the skills and knowledge for college. Out of this experiment grew the college's first study skills center aimed at helping low-achieving students build the skills they needed for college survival. A training program for local police was implemented with funds from the federal Law Enforcement Education Program.

These 1970s Aquinites flash the hippest style.

The Theater Department continued to stage productions like Brendan Behan's *The Hostage* (1971) in the Carriage House until the small theater was closed due to fire marshal concerns.

In the mid-1970s, the Athletic Department added its popular summer sports camps in baseball and basketball for area youth, taking advantage of its growing reputation in those sports. (Aquinas's baseball squad earned its first of several state titles in 1979.)

The result of this sometimes frenzied and frenetic activity was that Aquinas College, unlike many other small private schools, survived the tumultuous 1970s and entered the 1980s in the black. Undergraduate enrollment through the 1970s reached a plateau around 2,050 and in 1980 reached 2,883. Thanks to the mid-1970s inflation, tuition had gone from $620 per year to $3,555. Through bold entrepreneurship and strict budget watching under the bulldog eye of John O'Connor, director of business and finance, Aquinas College was no longer the small, focused Catholic liberal arts college it had been prior to Hruby's arrival. But how long could the creative energy and pace be sustained? And what would happen in the 1980s as Aquinas College's innovative programs for women, career changers, and seniors got copied by the larger and wealthier colleges in the area? And would the market for nontraditional-age degree completion continue as more eighteen-year-old women were completing their degrees before starting families? These strategic questions were important, but sometimes they overshadowed another fundamental question that longtime faculty were asking themselves: In its attempt to be all things to all people, was Aquinas losing its distinctive identity? Was the college risking a significant break from its tradition and past? Was there too much emphasis on nontraditional students? Had the college emphasized ecumenism at the expense of losing its focus on Catholicism? The mission statement developed for the 1977 North Central Accreditation visit said: "The mission of Aquinas College is to provide for a liberal-arts education with a career orientation in a Catholic, Christian context to all students capable of profiting from such an education regardless of their sex, age, religion, ethnic or racial background." To some, it seemed too broad.

As President Hruby rounded out his career at Aquinas, the institution had become "the little college that could," but past success was no guarantee of ongoing survival. Already on the horizon were warning signs of future stresses. The college still had no significant

Gala Weekend continued to offered festivity and entertainment in the 1980s.

Professor Thomas Dooley came to Aquinas in 1977 to introduce computers into the classrooms.

The beer tent became a Gala Weekend favorite. Here librarian Hiram Bakes tends bar.

At the beginning of the personal computing age, students helped students learn how to use the new technology.

Early computer students needed to learn BASIC and other programming languages.

Residence hall life was less formal than in the 1960s.

There was only one computer per residence hall.

Basketball great Laray Hardy's college-career scoring record of 2,642 points made him the most prolific scorer in Michigan. Here in 1986, he goes down court to score.

Women's basketball great Kathy Grzegorski led the Lady Saints to victory in the 1980s.

endowment and was heavily dependent on tuition to sustain itself from year to year. In addition, the "living endowment" of the Dominicans' contributed services was slowly eroding as teaching sisters retired without being replaced by younger nuns or priests because of the general drop in vocations. That meant that the college faculty would increasingly be composed of lay people, many of whom would not be Catholic or come from the Catholic educational tradition. These faculty members would have to be compensated at professional rates, with full benefits, which would have an ongoing impact on the college's finances. In addition, the buildings erected in the boom years 1955 to 1969 were aging and in need of continued maintenance. (Under Hruby's presidency—though significant restoration was done on Holmdene to transform it into an administration building and to turn the old stables into the pastoral center after a 1975 fire—only one new building was added to the campus, the Art and Music Center, opened in 1982.)

Other innovations came in the 1980s. In 1985, Gary Eberle was asked by Paul Nelson to develop the Insignis Program for Honors Students, and shortly after that a Child Development Center was started which eventually evolved into a charter school on the west side of Grand Rapids. One of the last of Hruby's innovations was to enact "age integration," streamlining the administration by erasing the lines between Continuing Education and traditional-age student education. But the pace of innovation slowed by the early 1980s as Hruby neared retirement. A three-day retreat was held at the Bay Inn at Harbor Springs in 1980, but, though the event served to

In the mid-1970s, the Tommies became the Saints by student choice after African-American athletes were taunted on the road for being "Toms."

The Art and Music Center was the only new building built during Norbert Hruby's presidency. Designed by Aquinas alumnus and architect Alfred Liu, its recital hall was underwritten by Ernest "Bud" Kretschmer.

rekindle the spirit of community among the Board members, faculty, staff, and students who attended, no great initiatives came out of the gathering, nothing, at any rate, like the explosion of new programs that emerged in the 1970s after the 1969 Self-Study and an earlier Harbor Springs retreat in 1973.

When he did retire, in 1986, President Hruby left behind a college that had tripled its enrollment through innovative programs tapping heretofore-untapped markets. Aquinas College had also become a prime mover in stabilizing the Eastown neighborhood, and had opened up to the world through a deliberately ecumenical strategy to become a more diverse, more eclectic community. Could this success continue?

Endnotes

1. Lee Jacokes,"A Brief Look Into the Past," 1975.
2. "Revolution at Aquinas," *Aquinas Magazine*, Summer 1969, 8.
3. Ibid., 10.
4. Ibid., 15.
5. Ibid., 16.
6. Ibid., 19.
7. *Historically Speaking*, disc 4.
8. Carl Pettersch,"Mobilizing Community Resources for Senior citizen Education Programs," Aquinas Archives.
9. Carl Pettersch,"Post-Retirement Feasiblity Study," 3. Aquinas Archives.
10. Linda Easley, Thomas Edison, Michael Williams. *Eastown!: A Report on how Aquinas College helped its local community reverse neighborhood transition and deterioration.* Grand Rapids: Aquinas College and W. K. Kellogg Foundation, 1978, 1.
11. "Notes on Neighborhood Meeting at Willowbrook, April 21, 1972." Aquinas Archives.
12. *Historically Speaking*, disc 4.

The new Art and Music Center provided more spacious studios for art classes than the cramped third floor of the Administration Building.

Professor John Teusink's pig anatomy quiz became legendary among biology students.

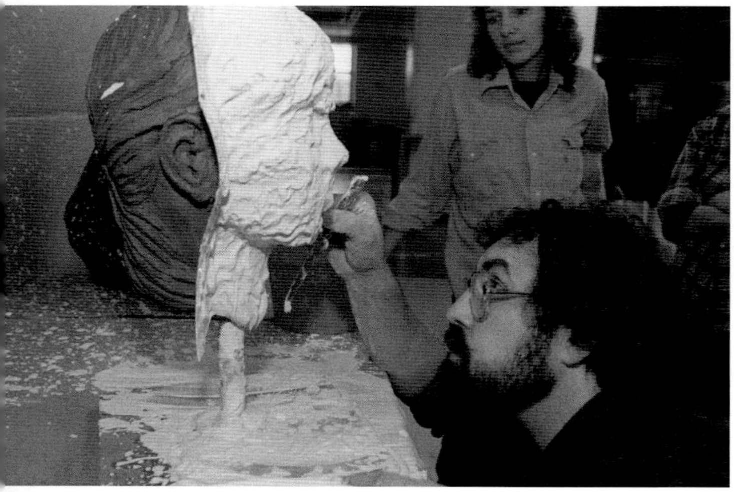

Sculptor Ron Pederson demonstrates the finer points of modeling with plaster.

ACADEMIC BUILDING
1607

A Campus for All Seasons

Aquinas College's campus was originally the estate of Edward and Susan Lowe. In 1905, they purchased what was then the McCoy dairy farm on the very outskirts of Grand Rapids. Lowe, a west Michigan lumber baron, was born in England and came to the United States with his parents, James and Eliza Butterworth Lowe.

The sixty-nine acres of the former estate are perched on a small, flat rise between two streams that run along the north and south sides of the property. The site for the manor house was selected above a ravine, and the house was designed by the Boston architectural firm Winslow and Bigelow. The Lowes named the estate *Holmdene*, an English place name that comes from the English *holm* oak plus the place name suffix *dene*, meaning "a wooded glade." The welcoming post on Robinson Road stills bears the name of the estate, though now only the original mansion is called Holmdene.

The campus buildings that date from the original Lowe family era are Holmdene, the Cook Carriage House, Bukowski Chapel (originally the stables), and Brink Hall (originally the family's winery).

After Edward and Susan Lowe died in the late 1930s, their heirs sold the property to the short-lived University of Grand Rapids, which went out of business during World War II, and the Dominican Sisters of Grand Rapids were able to secure a loan for $115,000 to purchase the land and buildings.

A surprising amount of wildlife can be found living on campus, from the abundant squirrels, to nocturnal raccoons and the occasional deer. Many species of birds live in the woodlots of the campus, including increasing numbers of red tail and other hawks, and barred owls. Geese, ducks, and herons can frequently be seen on the campus's three ponds.

As Aquinas has grown and added bricks and mortar in the years since buying the property in 1945, the college has tried to maintain the original feel of an English country estate, preserving the great variety of old growth trees, and becoming a mecca for grade school leaf collectors in the fall, as well as a semipublic "park" for many Grand Rapids neighbors who come to walk their dogs along the beautifully wooded paths, high school seniors who come to pose for their senior pictures, and for couples who come in droves on the weekends to have their wedding photos taken against the beautiful natural backdrop of this campus which was once named the most beautiful in Michigan.

Sister Mary Navarre, O.P., once said, "I think for me one of Aquinas's greatest strengths, in addition to the personalities of the past, is the setting. The woods are beautiful at all times of the year, and I was here in wintertime once, and met a woman cross-country skiing who had been skiing in Colorado, and she said this is as beautiful as any other place in the world. And the other day I was driving in and I saw a student over by the pond standing motionless staring out at the pond, and I looked in the direction of his stare and there was a heron, and I thought that in the midst of this bourgeoning city of Grand Rapids, Aquinas is an oasis of green, kind of quiet and peaceful, and thanks to Mr. Lowe who imported many distant trees and planted many trees, we have this exquisite campus. And I hope we can realize that this is our natural environment that really sets us apart and it's a special blessing, and I really think we need to preserve and treasure it. We are this oasis both in this area of greenery and academic excellence and a caring community. It sounds like an ad for Aquinas, but it's true."[1]

Endnote

1. *Historically Speaking*, disc 4.

FACULTY

HISTORIC
LANDMARK
No. 39
Aquinas College
Circa 1886
GRAND RAPIDS HISTORIC
PRESERVATION COMMISSION

AQUINAS COLLEGE

Baccalaureate & Commencement

THE HIGHLIGHT OF EACH ACADEMIC YEAR is commencement when students, faculty, staff, parents, and Board of Trustees gather to confer degrees on graduates. At Aquinas College, commencement is also a celebration of the core values of the college, with a senior awards ceremony on the night before commencement, a formal Baccalaureate Mass celebrated with the bishop at St. Andrew's Cathedral, and the academic commencement and conferral of honorary and earned degrees.

Emotions run high through the weekend as the graduates say farewell to their student days and proudly enter the ranks of Aquinas College alumni.

AQUINAS COLLEGE
GRAND RAPIDS • MICHIGAN

The Four Charisms

IN THE CATHOLIC TRADITION, charisms are gifts of grace given to us for the benefit of others. The four charisms of the Grand Rapids Dominicans and Aquinas College are prayer, study, service , and community.

PRAYER: Prayer, whether in formal liturgies, retreats, informal gatherings or regular Masses, fosters students' spiritual lives, and, along with study, forms the backbone of the Catholic intellectual tradition of *fides et ratio*, faith and reason.

STUDY: The intellectual and academic foundation students receive at Aquinas prepares them for professional careers and lives as contributing members of their communities. The course of study is rigorous but the rewards are great.

SERVICE: We are called to serve the world with our gifts of grace, whether the recipients of our service are down the hall or across the world. Aquinas students and alumni can point to a long tradition of service throughout the world since the school's founding days.

COMMUNITY: The Aquinas College community is comprised of faculty, staff, students, alumni, and friends of the college who experience life's joys and share life's sorrows in a spirit of love and mutual support.

PUMA

Chapter 6

Crisis and Recovery 1986–1997

A nationwide search for a new president, led by Joseph Parini, chairman of the Board of Trustees, brought Dr. Peter D. O'Connor from Incarnate Word College in San Antonio, Texas, to Aquinas in the summer of 1986. When he arrived, he looked forward to implementing many of the visions he had for how a small liberal arts college should be run. He also set out to address some of the longstanding needs of the college as he saw them. In an interview conducted after his departure from the college, O'Connor recalled, "I wanted to build on the strengths that I thought Dr. Hruby had contributed to the college. I saw it as a very fine school and I wanted to preserve that strength. I thought it had some needs that I might be able to address, and that included things like facilities and faculty development, clarification of the sense of the mission of the college."[1]

Faculty and staff quickly noticed changes in the campus environment. Much of the financial success of the Hruby years was built on innovative new programs combined with a fairly strict and sometimes austere budget. One of the budget-saving measures was deferred maintenance on buildings and grounds.

Under the direction of President O'Connor and Sister Nathalie Meyer, vice president of administration, the college set about an ambitious program of repair, upgrading, and construction. Old sidewalks and roofs were replaced, and underground fiber-optic cable was laid in anticipation of the coming computer revolution. Albertus Magnus Hall of Science was renovated with a grant from the Grand Rapids Foundation. In 1987, the college purchased Christopher House, a large house on Robinson Road that the diocese had used for a time as a seminary. The building was renovated for new programs. Changes in technology drove some of the activity. In 1988, a campuswide high-tech IBM ROLM telephone system was installed introducing students and faculty to phone mail. In October 1988, the Computer Department began the yearlong installation of the Colleague computer software system for maintaining student academic records and administrative computing functions.

The biggest change by far, however, was the addition of eleven new buildings resulting from the $6 million purchase of the Reformed Bible College, a small religious school on the east boundary of the campus whose property extended to Woodward Lane. The sudden acquisition, which was approved by the Board of Trustees, stunned everyone. The acquisition of the RBC campus was initiated by Dr. O'Connor in a private conversation with Reformed Bible College President Edwin D. Roels. In July 1988, officials of the Bible College and Aquinas mutually agreed to the terms of a contract, and that fall Aquinas students were already occupying some former RBC residence halls.

President Peter O'Connor increased the size of campus with the purchase of the nearby Reformed Bible College property.

The growth spurt continued. In spring 1989, O'Connor unveiled an ambitious master plan for the campus. The plan would have revolutionized the look of the forty-year-old Robinson Road campus. A dramatic new Fulton Street entrance was planned with a dream of spanning the ravine with a suspension bridge to bring visitors through the most beautiful part of campus. At the heart of campus, directly across from Holmdene would be a freestanding library, long a dream of Aquinas planners. The buildings and property of the former Reformed Bible College would be used for residence halls, classrooms, a conference center, and additional parking space for the anticipated bulge in enrollment.

Such enormous physical changes would come with a high price tag, and in 1989, the school kicked off an $8 million capital campaign called "Aquinas Grows,"

The purchase of the Reformed Bible College campus gained Aquinas more buildings and residence halls, but the cost of the campus stretched the college's budget to the breaking point.

The former Reformed Bible College campus is formally claimed by Aquinas College and the property is rechristened the East Campus. Timmer Hall, in the background, was demolished to make way for Jarecki Center and later the Hauenstein Library.

Professor Lee Jacokes leads a strategic planning session in 1992. The college's ambitious plans had to be put on hold due to a major financial crisis.

This statue of the young scholar Thomas Aquinas was sculpted on campus by Sister Phyllis Mrozinski and dedicated in 1989.

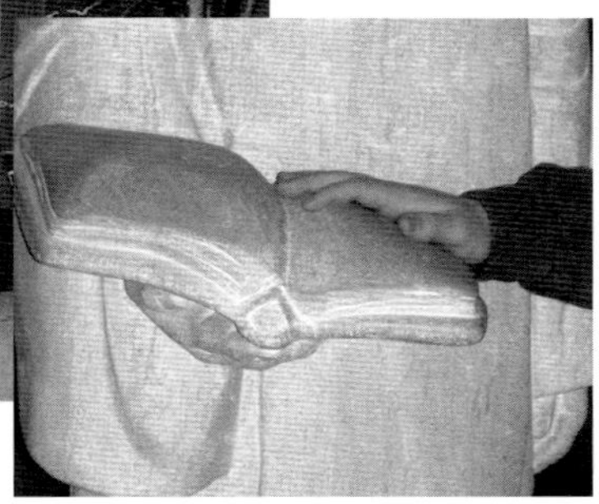

Folklore among students says that if you rub Thomas's book before an exam, you will get an A. The stone is worn smooth.

headed by Dr. Frank Bruno, former academic vice president, now director of development. Before the capital campaign could accomplish its goal, however, a major financial crisis arose. The late 1980s saw the advent of the "baby bust," a time when there was the smallest pool of eighteen-year-olds since the Second World War. Enrollments, instead of rising as O'Connor had anticipated, declined precipitously as students were lured away to lower-priced state universities. In addition, debt service from the loans used to purchase the Reformed Bible College campus added significantly to the college's financial burden. The situation only grew worse when, two years in a row, accounting oversights led to operating deficits in excess of $1 million. The college entered a period of financial belt-tightening. In retrospect, it was easy to see that the euphoric spate of building, renovation, and acquisition had come at a high cost.

The Board of Trustees had made its decision to move forward with the expenditures and the purchase of the Bible College property based on financial projections that grossly overestimated enrollment projections during the 1990s. Given the demographics and the growing competition from state universities like Grand Valley, Western Michigan, and Central Michigan who were all establishing campuses in Grand Rapids, Aquinas was losing its grip on the continuing education market it had dominated in the 1970s. In addition, the projected income from the use of Donnelly Center as a conference center was overestimated. The debts that had been incurred came at an extremely high rate of interest. The college suddenly found itself about $15 million in debt, and the interest became a crippling part of the yearly budget.

The effects were felt all over campus. Many on campus, especially faculty, felt somewhat vindicated in the sense that they had been questioning almost from the start whether the college could afford the sudden burst of expenditure after decades of fiscal austerity. In an attempt to salvage the budget, staff members had to be let go, and faculty were offered

The addition of an office tower to Albertus Magnus Hall of Science gave faculty additional space but added to the college's debt burden.

incentives to retire. It was clear that the financial hardship would last for years.

With spiraling debt and falling enrollment, Aquinas seemed headed for serious trouble, if not collapse. Then, in March 1990, President O'Connor abruptly requested that the Aquinas College Board of Trustees grant him a medical leave of absence from the presidency because of a back problem that required serious and disabling surgery. R. Paul Nelson, then dean of student development, was appointed to act as interim president. The announcement took everyone, including Nelson, by surprise. Nelson recalls how he was summoned to Browne Center to meet with Raymond Knape, chairman of the Board of Trustees. Nelson wondered if the summons had to do with his not rehiring the college's basketball coach a few days before, but when he arrived he also found former President Hruby and Sister Aquinas Weber there. Hruby, who had worked closely with Nelson for over twenty years, mumbled to him, "Lightning is about to strike," and Nelson feared the worst. When he walked into the office where Knape waited, however, Knape explained the situation to him and asked him to take over as acting president.

President R. Paul Nelson, who had served Aquinas in many capacities since 1969, replaced Peter O'Connor and served as president until his retirement in 1997.

"What went through my mind," Nelson later recalled, "was 'Don't just walk out of here, run! Because this is something that you don't want to take on.' But I really had a sense of calling, unlike I've ever had before, that this is something I should do. So I, perhaps too quickly, said, 'Yes, I'll do it,' thinking that it would be on an interim basis for six months or so."[2] In April, President O'Connor officially tendered his resignation to the Board of Trustees, and a Search Committee was appointed to replace him. Eventually, the search was suspended and the Board of Trustees asked Paul Nelson to become the fourth president of Aquinas College, a job he held until 1997.

In the few years he was with Aquinas, O'Connor had overseen the development of a five-year strategic plan, increased financial aid to students, and, most significantly, purchased the seventeen-acre Reformed Bible College campus. The "Aquinas Grows" campaign, in the end, was only able to raise $6 million towards its $8 million goal. With the perspective of twenty years, the expansion of the campus to Woodward Lane through the purchase of the RBC property enabled the college to grow. The new property eventually provided room for a soccer field and new housing, and enabled the college to achieve its long-held dream of building a large freestanding library. The price paid and the gamble taken were both very steep, however. The job of Nelson and his staff was to rally the college back to its original mission and to steer it safely through years when its very existence hung in the balance.

Meanwhile . . .

Although the dramatic financial crisis and the events surrounding O'Connor's resignation captured the focus during the late 1980s and early 1990s, the main business of Aquinas College, providing students with a first-rate education, went on. In 1986, the Education Department began its master's program in education, which swelled to great proportions in the 1990s as Aquinas's reputation as an educator of teachers grew throughout Michigan. In 1987, the North Central Accrediting Association gave the college a ten-year approval with no focus visits, and in 1991 the Spectrum Scholarship Program was begun to encourage high-

The refurbished Browne Center became home to the Education Department and the Emeritus College.

achieving high school students to enroll in Aquinas. Albertus Hall was renovated in 1989 and was rededicated with a gala reception in September of that year, and that same year Aquinas celebrated twenty years of being one of the leaders in Continuing Education. The Emeritus Program headquarters, by then housed in the former Christopher House, got a facelift thanks to a generous grant from Robert W. Browne, and the building, which also became the location of the Education Department, was renamed Browne Center. In 1987, a weeklong celebration of the feast of St. Thomas Aquinas in late January quickly became a college tradition replete with performances of medieval theater by the students of the Insignis Program, faculty teaching in caps and gowns, a special Dean's List Mass, and an annual St. Thomas lecture by a distinguished theologian or scholar. The Women's Center was founded in the late 1980s, and a Child Development Center was begun in 1989. The distinguished astronomer and businessman Ralph B. Baldwin donated $30,000 towards a new observatory to be constructed on the roof of Albertus Hall, a project that was dedicated in 1992. In 1994, another generous gift from Baldwin provided funds for installing an eighteen-inch telescope under the dome. A special arrangement with nearby Blodgett Hospital gained the college's medical neighbors a new parking lot and

Rabbi Albert Lewis, longtime director of the Emeritus Program, teaches a class in Browne Center.

A generous gift from local businessman and astronomer Ralph Baldwin allowed for the building of an observatory atop Albertus Magnus Hall of Science.

Aquinas a new soccer field in the heart of campus to attract athletes to the nation's fastest growing collegiate sport.

"First Light" is the phrase used in astronomical circles for the inauguration of a new telescope. The Baldwin Observatory's eighteen-inch telescope was first used September 21, 1994.

President Nelson

In spring 1991, the Presidential Search Committee officially asked Paul Nelson to become president of Aquinas College. As Board member and Aquinas alumnus Ned Smith recalls, "Paul was the perfect choice for the presidency at the time. We were hurting badly in many many ways and Paul was the answer. His integrity is above reproach, his love of the college is there, and everybody knew it. We needed someone like Paul, and we couldn't have found anyone better than Paul. I think he fit the bill perfectly." Given the seriousness of the time, Nelson forewent the elaborate presidential inauguration ceremony of his predecessor and opted instead for a Mass of Blessing attended by the campus community and celebrated by Bishop Robert Rose. The simplicity and sincerity of the service set the tone for his presidency.

The first and most pressing challenge Nelson faced was the college's $15 million debt. His first goal was

A hallmark of President Nelson's style was his easy interaction with students.

Masses for large gatherings were held in the Wege Center Ballroom.

to try to slow down spending, so tight belts got even tighter. Next, he and his team worked on refinancing the large debt so that it could be paid off over a longer term at a lower interest rate. Bonds were issued, and the immediate threat of being financially overwhelmed was allayed, but financial struggle became the hallmark of Nelson's seven years in office. Years later, Nelson commented, "With so much money committed simply to debt service, the college lost the investment capital it needed to spur innovation and creativity."[3] The decision was made to funnel as much money as possible to traditional-age student enrollment and retention, which was seen as the long-term survival strategy for the college. Sister Maureen Geary, vice president for finance, worked with Nelson to construct realistic budgets and oversee costs, and by the mid-1990s annual budgets were balanced again thanks to what Nelson called "heroic efforts of faculty and staff to do their jobs and to do them very well" in spite of the austerity called for.

In fact, much creative work did take place in those years. The faculty plunged ahead with a sweeping curriculum reform that consumed over five years of planning and implementation. In part, the reform was a reaction against the 1970s-style cafeteria approach to general education that had been so innovative twenty years before. In 1998, the Academic Assembly passed a proposal to develop a Freshman Humanities Program. The idea for the program arose as the result of concerns voiced by faculty members that students were entering college without sufficient knowledge of history and general education, and without adequate skills to get the most out of their college work. The Humanities Program's development was guided by Sister Marie Celeste Miller, and it was designed to combine a study of western and world humanities with the development of skills in reading, writing, and public speaking. Dr. Daniel Brooks of the English Department, who later became longtime head of the program, notes that when it was introduced it was the only core course students had to take. The course was challenging academically, crammed with information about the art, literature, music, and philosophy of the world. All of this was leavened, in the early years, with the fun of the annual Greek games. Individual classes competed with one another in some of the traditional Greek Olympic games and in some invented ones like the chariot race whose horses were other students and whose chariots were constructed of fifty-gallon plastic drums on wheels. Dr. Michael Blomme of the Chemistry Department appeared as Zeus and Sister Katrina Hartman impersonated the goddess Athena. Along with other deities and students in togas, the day turned into a fun event for all.

The Greek Games became part of the Humanities Program tradition for a number of years in the 1990s.

The new freshman course proved a success. In its second year, its potential was recognized by a National Endowment for the Humanities grant for faculty development, and by 1993 that experience led the faculty to begin to implement other core courses. For two-years the faculty met, argued, compromised, and finally implemented new core requirements. It was the first major curriculum overhaul since the 1970s. A new freshman experience, "Inquiry and Expression," would serve the needs of first-year students while humanities became a second-year course. In their third year, students would take a theology course, and in the fourth year a "Global Explorations and Meaning" course would provide students with a global worldview. The college was a long way from the large and tightly restricted core requirements of the 1950s, but faculty began to notice changes in students as a result. The emphasis on communication and research skills early in their careers prepared students for upper division work, and having a common experience with shared knowledge enabled instructors to presuppose a certain knowledge base among students.

Another major adjustment to education occurred in the 1990s as personal computers and the computer revolution swept campus. A $350,000 grant from the Grand Rapids Foundation allowed the library to automate its circulation system, and that was only the beginning of the computerization of campus and of higher education generally.

The Education Department remained a site of considerable innovation. In 1988, the "Master in the Art of Teaching" degree was created to offer advanced studies for classroom teachers. In 1990, Aquinas was selected as a site for the Learning Styles Network Base, and in 1992 the college was named a Midwest Teaching and Learning Center. These programs, run by Dr. Katy Lux, gave Aquinas's education program a national profile. In 1993, the Education Department added an innovative master of education degree combined with an initial certification program aimed at adults in other professions who might want to change careers into teaching.

A grant from the Kellogg Foundation allowed the Learning Resources Center, as the library was then known, to computerize and automate its operations in 1991, doing away with the need for a card catalog. Here librarian Jeanine Weber happily dumps the old cards.

The human chess match sponsored by the Fencing Club was held during Gala Weekend.

Not every attempt at new programming in those years met with equal success. A proposal for an Aquinas College law school died in its initial phases of planning, and The Weekend College, a plan to offer degree completion programs in a Friday, Saturday, and Sunday format was vigorously opposed by an already overtaxed faculty.

A Changing of the Guard

During the Nelson years, many faculty members achieved landmarks. Notable among the longtime faculty who retired were Ken Marin from the Economics Department, Sister Marybride Ryan and Betty Jennings from the English Department, Sister Marie Joseph Ryan from the History Department, and Eugene Hopkins from the Music Department. Larry Blovits, well-known portrait painter, retired from the Art Department to pursue his art full-time, and Ralph J. Bennett, known to students and faculty alike as R. J., also retired. Bennett was given an honorary degree from Aquinas at the 1993 commencement to recognize his contributions to the college, especially in Continuing Education. Coach Terry Bocian earned his eight-hundredth career baseball victory, and in 1995 longtime Physical Education faculty members Ernie Mousseau, Betty Taylor, and Lenore

Kalenda retired, along with psychology professor Jerry Heckenmuller, and sociology professor Sister Nancy Flummerfelt. Faculty members John "Doc" Poje and Dennis Burfeindt passed away during these years. These landmarks, along with the 1989 death of Monsignor Bukowski, marked a significant break with the past. Some of these retiring faculty members, like Ken Marin and Sister Jean Milhaupt, had been students at the old

Incoming 1990 freshmen get enthused about Aquinas during orientation week.

Aquinas College. In their lifetimes, Aquinas grew from a tiny school in downtown Grand Rapids to a nationally known four-year college, ranked in the second tier of Midwest colleges by *U.S. News and World Report*.

Service

A hallmark of Nelson's presidency was a reemphasis on the Dominican charisms of prayer, study, service, and community. In 1990, using the new residence houses on Woodward Lane, the college initiated the idea of "service houses," in which student groups could petition to live in the apartment-like residences in exchange for undertaking a yearlong service project. The idea for the program was generated by Brad Winkler, dean of students, based on similar houses at the College of Wooster, in Ohio, and other schools across the country. The idea caught on quickly, and student groups competed with each other to live in them. Students needed to present a service proposal

World affairs continued to be a concern as these 1991 students prepare to protest the Gulf War.

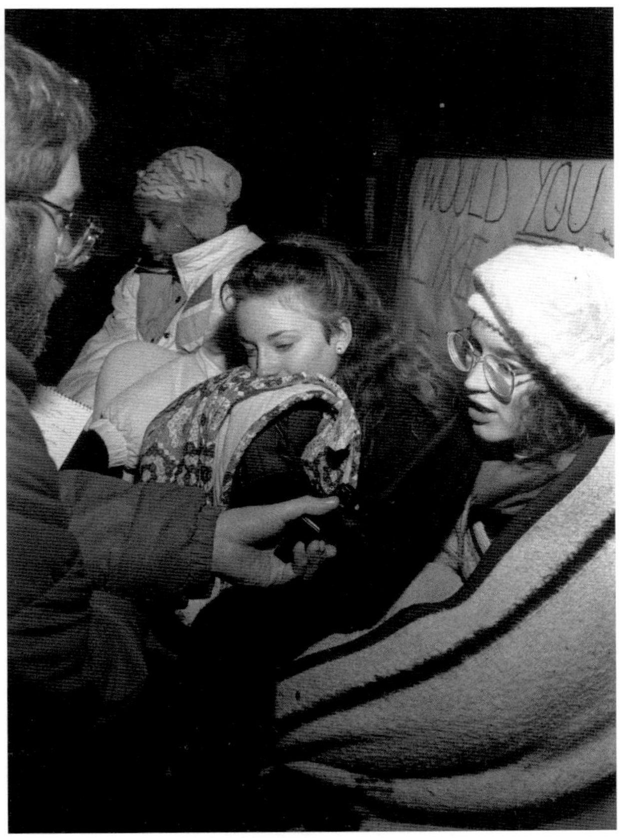
Students camp out in winter in cardboard boxes on Wege Mall in 1991 to call attention to the plight of the homeless.

in the spring of the year about their service plan. An orphanage in Peru, local environmental groups, and many other organizations and causes have been the beneficiaries of the students' service ethic.

The Aquinas ethic of service also led to the development of extended service trips to Haiti, Oaxaca (Mexico), and to various locations within the United States like Appalachia and New Orleans. It became very rare, in those years, for students to graduate without having some sort of service work as part of their college experience. Stella Ferris, the enthusiastic multicultural director in those years, recalled the transformative power of a service learning trip to Haiti for students and their advisors who worked with Mother Teresa's sisters at a hospital for children with AIDS. "I and three Aquinas students witnessed, and saw, and held two babies that died. I had never, myself, been challenged like that, and there was a moment where you had to get control about, this is what I am supposed to be doing, and at the same time you had to turn around to the students and be a mentor to them and say, 'Okay, let's pull it together, we're here for a purpose.'"[4]

A student-led campaign to renovate the Carriage House led to a renovated student center in 1995. Shortly after, the Moose Café, a full-service coffee bar opened.

Yes, the Moose Café comes with a moose.

In the early 1990s, the Social Action Committee sponsored events to raise awareness of homelessness and hunger with Third-World Dinners and camp outs in cardboard boxes on Wege Mall in winter. Students traveled to Washington, D.C., to demonstrate against apartheid in South Africa, and they were in the forefront, twenty years after the first Earth Day, in getting the campus to increase recycling.

One 1990s anecdote among many provides evidence of Aquinas's continuous tradition of service. During a trip to Appalachia in the Nelson years, a few students were helping clean up a church after a flood, and, in talking to the nuns who ran the church, they discovered that that very building had been constructed with the help of Monsignor Bukowski and Aquinas students some thirty years before.

In addition to service, students were busy reviving a campus radio station, WAQU, staging Black History Month plays, and establishing the multicultural group J.A.M.M.I.N. Students led the drive to reopen the carriage house as a student center, after it had been closed for more than twenty years because of theater fire code restrictions. Used in the interim for storage, the carriage house was transformed in a $300,000 renovation and the Cook Carriage House quickly became a hub of student life, offering concerts, a full service coffee shop, poetry readings, and a variety of entertainments.

Sports teams continued to shine. In the mid-1990s, the baseball team won three consecutive state championships. In 1990, softball, under coach Mary Takas won the state championship and qualified for the nationals for the first time in college history. Tennis, track and field, and cross-country continued to earn berths in national tournaments. In the mid-1990s women's soccer coach Shannon Besette made Aquinas into a powerhouse in the Wolverine Hoosier Athletic Conference.

Coach Mary Takas took Aquinas's softball teams to new heights, winning the state title in 1990.

Logging On

During the 1990s, the world outside academia was being transformed by the computer revolution, and Aquinas struggled to keep abreast of the new technology. The college had to keep pace with the proliferation of personal computers as well as the computer-savvy incoming students. The old Burroughs system that the college had used through the 1980s was severely limited in the new environment. Increased space was given to computers, and in the early 1990s a computer classroom was unveiled for the Mathematics Department and soon text and training labs occupied nearly one-half of the Academic Building's third floor. Classroom and office applications required constant training as new hardware and software came on line.

Significant Gifts

Throughout the 1990s, Aquinas alumni and friends continued to be generous. In December 1996, longtime Board of Trustees member and friend of the college Peter Wege donated an unprecedented gift of $5 million worth of Steelcase Corporation stock to be added to the college endowment. It was the largest single gift in the history of the college to that date. Wege, who once served as director of development for the college, said, "In the next five to ten years, I hope to see the school reach new plateaus, and I think we'll see this school become one of the finest small Catholic colleges in the country." The following year, Steelcase Corporation announced the public sale of its stock and the value of Wege's gift increased considerably. This substantial gift seemed to provide the financial cushion Aquinas needed to stabilize itself fiscally and to look ahead with optimism.

In 1996, an unprecedented gift of $5 million worth of Steelcase Corporation stock from longtime college benefactor Peter Wege promised to relieve the financial burden of the college.

Visitors to campus can stroll through a scale-size replica of the Solar System using the Foster Planet Walk.

The Contemporary Writers Series, begun in 1997 by alumni Tony Foster and his wife Linda Nemec Foster, brings well-known authors to campus several times a year. Here Nobel Prize–winning poet Seamus Heaney reads in the 2005–06 season.

On the lighter, somewhat whimsical side, art professor Ron Pederson and physics professor Charles Frydrych designed a scale model of the solar system to be used as an outdoor instruction aid. Alumnus Dr. Tony Foster came forward with funding for the project. Now students and visitors can follow the Foster Planet Walk through campus. Beginning at the center of the "solar system," Albertus Hall, they can stroll from planet to planet and find nine large fieldstones, each of which bears a cast metal replica of the planet it represents.

At Paul Nelson's retirement, the college inaugurated its mascot, a "Saint" Bernard, which is named Nelson.

Foster and his wife, poet Linda Nemec Foster, were also instrumental in creating another longstanding feature of the college, the Contemporary Writers Series. Each year since 1996, four nationally and internationally known writers have come to campus to present readings of their work and creative writing workshops for students.

Feeling he had achieved his main goal of stabilizing the college after the unsettling years of the late 1980s and early 1990s, Paul Nelson announced in spring of 1996 that he would step down from the presidency in 1997. While virtually all members of the college respected his decision, most were sad to see him go. All agreed that he had been the right man for the difficult times. The commitment to the holistic education of students that he demonstrated throughout his career at Aquinas—from his years with Continuing Education through his tenure as dean of student development, and in his presidency—represented the best of the Aquinas tradition. At his retirement, many events were held in Nelson's honor. Students proclaimed April 24, 1997, as Paul Nelson Day, and the school's spirit mascot—a costume of a large St. Bernard dog—was christened "Nelson" in his honor. A large retirement party was given for Nelson at the Amway Grand Plaza Hotel at which Paul was presented with the statues of the two stone lions that sit in front of the New York Public Library. They were meant to remind him of the two stone lions that keep guard over the front door of Holmdene, but, more importantly, they are named "Patience" and "Fortitude," two qualities that Nelson exhibited many times over during his years at the college.

With a year's advance warning, the Board of Trustees formed a Search Committee to find Nelson's replacement. In focus group after focus group, faculty, staff, students, and supporters of the college insisted the new president must have good fundraising skills. Given the recent history of the college, that should have come as no surprise. The college was at a critical point in its history and much rode on the selection of a new leader. Over a several month period, the Search Committee sifted through over eighty resumes from qualified candidates, and by February 1997, they were ready to bring three finalists to campus. In the end, the selection fell to Dr. Harry J. Knopke, then vice president for student affairs at the University of Alabama, Birmingham, Medical School.

As the college approached the end of the twentieth century, it found itself radically changed from what it had been. Yet, one thing remained constant through all the transformations: the Dominican emphasis on prayer, study, service, and community. In what new directions would those four charisms take the college in the new millennium?

Endnotes

1. Historically Speaking, disc 5. The material in this chapter is largely a transcript of disk 5 of the oral history of Aquinas College compiled by the college's Historical Commission in 1997.
2. Ibid.
3. Ibid.
4. Ibid.

Chapter 7

Into the New Millennium 1997–2011

The college that greeted President Harry Knopke in 1997 had just been through a painful period of recovery and, through great sacrifice by faculty and staff, had stabilized itself by a return to its core mission, providing a liberal arts education rooted in the Catholic and Dominican intellectual tradition.

Even though the number of sisters working at the college was declining, the connection with the past was kept alive by staff members who been teaching and administering at the school since the days of Monsignor Bukowski. In 1995, the Aquinas College Historical Commission was founded by the Board with the mission to increase awareness of the college's history among faculty, students, and staff. The Historical Commission almost immediately set out to collect hundreds of hours of taped interviews with retired Aquinas College alumni, staff, and faculty which were edited and then released as *Historically Speaking,* a set of five hour-long compact disks. In addition, Commission members created a comprehensive Heritage and Traditions web site that included highlights of the college's history along with photos and sound clips from the oral history tapes. To emphasize the Dominican heritage of the college,

President Knopke led the development of a new mission statement in 2001:

Aquinas College, an inclusive educational community rooted in the Catholic Dominican tradition, provides a liberal arts education with a global perspective, emphasizes career preparation focused on leadership and service to others, and fosters a commitment to lifelong learning dedicated to the pursuit of truth and the common good.[1]

As the past was being tended to, however, the future beckoned. In 1997, the college welcomed the largest incoming freshman class in its history (until then).

Under the leadership of President Knopke, the college embarked on a spate of new programs and a construction plan that rivaled the building boom years of the 1950s and 1960s. In 1998, the first newly built residence halls since the 1960s were opened. The three Ravine Apartments provided living space for up to 108 upper-class students. In 1999, the $7 million Jarecki Center for Advanced Learning was opened to house the

The opening of the Grace Hauenstein Library in 2006 realized the college's long-deferred dream of having a state-of-the-art freestanding library.

Business and Graduate Management Programs. In 2000, the Board of Trustees authorized a unique collaboration between Aquinas College, Circle Theater and the Catholic Secondary Schools that, after a period of fundraising, led to the opening of the new Performing Arts Center in 2003 with an Aquinas College production of Thornton Wilder's *Our Town*. The college theater program would utilize the state-of-the-art performance center during the academic year while Circle Theater community theater would pack the seats in the summer time, and the Catholic high schools would stage musicals and plays in it during the fall and spring breaks of the college.

President Harry J. Knopke oversaw the college's second building boom with the creation of the Performing Arts Center, Jarecki Center for Advanced Learning, and the new library planning.

At the same time that the traditional majors continued to thrive, new academic programs were developed that continued the college's long commitment to service. In 1997, a master's degree in science education was developed by the School of Education. A Nursing Program was established in collaboration with University of Detroit-Mercy, and the "Conductive Education/POHI (Physically Impaired or Otherwise Handicapped Individuals)" major became the first program in the United States to offer professional training in the Hungarian-based comprehensive education program for children with motor disabilities.[2] The Community Leadership Program was instituted to develop leaders for nonprofit organizations, offering a unique combination of interdisciplinary courses to provide a

foundation in administration, organizational leadership, and analytical problem solving.[3] A new major in athletic training was added, and a sustainable business major was added in fall of 2003. This interdisciplinary major integrates science, business, and environmental studies and became the first undergraduate program in the United States to focus on sustainable business practices. (A "Masters in Sustainable Business" was added in 2010). The Center for Sustainability was founded to be a resource for the college and businesses on sustainable practices and new developments in the field of sustainability.

Established programs achieved landmarks in these years. In 2003, the Ireland Program in Tully Cross

The addition of the Ravine Apartments brought new on-campus living spaces for juniors and seniors.

The opening of the Jarecki Center for Advanced Learning in 1999 brought the campus a fully "plugged in" building ready for twenty-first century technology. Here benefactors Peter Wege, left, and Clare Jarecki connect the symbolic power cord.

A unique collaboration among Aquinas College, Community Circle Theatre, and Catholic Secondary Schools made the new Performing Arts Center possible. Opened in 2003, the PAC is rarely dark, being used by the college and the Catholic High Schools during the academic year and Circle Theatre during the summer.

The Aquinas theater tradition continues in the new Performing Arts Center with several plays a year.

marked its thirtieth anniversary, and the Contemporary Writers Series celebrated ten years in 2007. The Women's Center was renamed the Jane Hibbard Idema Women's Studies Center after the well-known women's advocate and former director of the college's Encore Program and Emeritus College. In 2005, the Insignis Program for Honors Students celebrated twenty-five years, and in 2008 the Emeritus College received a $1.2 million grant from the Osher Foundation, changed its name to the Osher Lifelong Learning Institute, and continued to offer a wide range of courses of interest to mature adult students.

President Knopke's commitment to community and world engagement led to increased offerings in international programs to include language and cultural immersion semesters abroad in Spain, France, Costa Rica, and Germany. In addition, he started the Woodrick Institute for the Study of Racism and Diversity, an organization later transferred to Grand Rapids Community College. The college also established the Sustainability Compact with the City of Grand Rapids and area educational institutions to encourage sustainable practices and share best practices. The Service Learning Program continued to be emphasized with the appointment of a full-time director and, for a while, a general education requirement for service or foreign study to encourage global learning. On Knopke's watch, Aquinas entered the charter school market with the opening of the Grand Rapids Child Discovery Center located in the old St. Adelbert's School on the west side. This collaboration between the college and Grand Rapids Public Schools brought the Reggio-Emilia method of education to west Michigan.

In June 2006, after his nine years at Aquinas and thirty-five years in higher education, Knopke retired from the presidency of the college to pursue new challenges bringing clean water and sanitation technologies to developing countries. During Knopke's nine years as president, Aquinas College consistently received rankings in the upper tier of Midwest colleges from the annual *U.S. News and World Report* ranking of colleges, but students best remember Knopke for the many interactions he and his wife Sheila had with them, including monthly dinners at Willowbrook, the president's house, for outstanding students, leaders, and faculty. His courses in medical ethics and his history tours of the South with students remain fond memories for both Knopke and his students.

Former Provost C. Edward Balog became Aquinas College's sixth president in 2006. Balog reemphasized the college's liberal arts core and Catholic and Dominican tradition that gave it its birth.

At Knopke's departure, the Board of Trustees named Provost C. Edward Balog, who had come to Aquinas in 2000, as interim president. After a one-year search for a new president, during which Balog had thrown his hat in the ring, the Board named him president, a title he assumed on July 1, 2006. Balog, a former history professor and longtime administrator at liberal arts colleges like Aquinas, felt his mission was to reemphasize both the liberal arts core of the academic program and the Catholic Dominican connection that made Aquinas unique.

In his years as provost, Balog had focused on enhancing the academic standing and quality of the existing programs and to foster programs, like Sustainable Business. Also high on his agenda was the hiring of young faculty with outstanding academic credentials to ensure the ongoing quality of education offered by Aquinas. In his "President's Message" in the spring 2009 edition of *Aquinas* magazine, Balog stressed the continuity and relevance of the kind of education Aquinas College offers its students. "The Dominican charisms of prayer, service, community, and learning are central to our mission; they are embedded in our curriculum. Within the broad reach of Catholic values, all our students engage in some kind of community service project, whether for credit in a service learning course or as a volunteer through a student organization. This sense of service and community is a practice and habit that can be nurtured and extended throughout a lifetime. We take seriously the fact that we are named for St. Thomas Aquinas, the great teacher. Thomas devoted his life to study and the pursuit of truth, and this is the same sense of commitment and persistence we instill in our students."[4]

Balog's and the college's confidence in the core liberal arts mission of the college was rewarded by several years of record-breaking incoming freshman classes. Significant efforts towards retaining these students once they arrived led to five consistent years of budget surpluses. That and significant gifts to the endowment led to a kind of financial stability that the college had not known for nearly twenty years. Balog believes "It is important from time to time for us to recognize what we do well. What we as a private college do well is to provide a quality education to a large portion of the population which might not otherwise have access, or resources, or the assistance needed to succeed.... I believe that our alumni and friends remain committed to the value of an Aquinas education and that we will continue to be among the leaders of American higher education."[5]

President Ed Balog's inauguration was celebrated with a campuswide "Viva Balog" party.

The most spectacular addition to the physical plant in these years was the opening of the $6.8 million Grace Hauenstein Library in fall 2006. The design of the library was completed by Progressive AE of Grand Rapids and made innovative use of the already-existing Jarecki Center, with its photo-voltaic roof, and added a dramatic inverted glass pyramid to house the library's book collection. The building was the first building on campus to receive silver LEED certification from the U.S. Green Building Council.

On January 19, 2011, Balog announced his retirement from the presidency, opening the door for a Board-led presidential search to replace him. In his eleven years with the college as provost and president, he created a legacy of academic excellence and a new level of professionalism among the faculty. Students who were here for his inauguration in 2006 will never forget the "Viva, Balog!" party, neatly book-ended by the Saint's banner headline of the announcement, "Hasta la Vista, Balog."

The story of Aquinas College is far from over. The college is building for its future. In fall 2010, the old Physical Education and Assembly Building, built in 1969, underwent a multi-million dollar overhaul to become the Sturrus Sports & Fitness Center, complete with renovated playing floor, new classrooms and offices, and a professional grade workout center. In 2010–2011, the Board of Trustees developed "Vision Twenty20: Creating a Habit of Mind." This strategic plan

The refurbished fieldhouse, now the Sturrus Sports & Fitness Center, provides professional level workout equipment for the use of all students, faculty, and staff.

highlighted financial stability, academic innovation, and Dominican and Catholic identity among its chief goals. The implementation of this plan will set the tone of the college for the upcoming ten years at least, and will provide a sense of direction as Aquinas moves into the future.

In many, if not most, ways, the college barely resembles the humble Novitiate Normal School that was its origin, any more than the rest of world resembles the world of 1886. We live in a truly global society, interconnected in ways unimaginable in the late nineteenth century. The sisters who founded the Normal School traveled by horse and buggy and their main teaching aids consisted of a few books and pieces of chalk. In the middle years of the twentieth century, the student body was homogenized and thoroughly Catholic. Today, the college has a diverse faculty and student body, and through the Internet has instant contact with cultural and educational resources that deliver the world to them in an instant.

The effort of remembering and passing on Aquinas College's values and traditions belongs to the present generation. Aquinas is one of nineteen Dominican colleges and universities in the United States. Because of the decline in religious vocations in the past thirty years, many if not all of them are facing a future in which the Dominicans' physical presence on campus will be dwindling, if not disappearing. In the 1990s, these colleges began sending faculty, staff, and students to Fanjeaux, a small town in the south of France where St. Dominic founded the first congregation of the Order of Preachers. There, participants learn the history of the founding of the Dominicans and discuss how their colleges can continue to live out the Dominican charisms in the contemporary world. Aquinas has been participating in the Fanjeaux Program since 1998, and it is hoped that through this program and commemorative activities like this history volume and the 125th anniversary celebration, the distinctive charisms of prayer, study, service, and community will guide Aquinas College's development long into the future. These core values have been the soul and motivating force of Aquinas College since its origins, and will continue to guide it into the future.

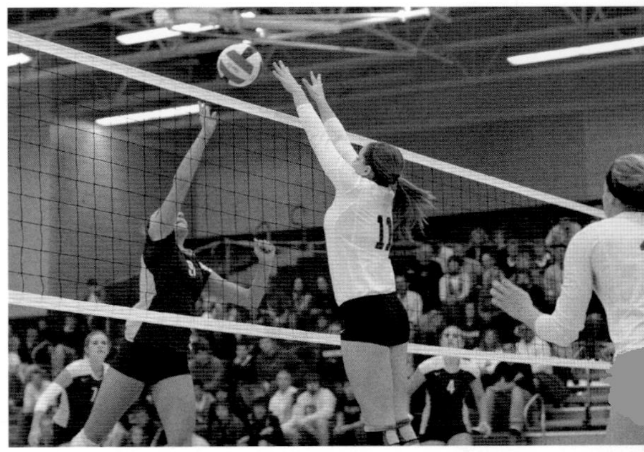

The Saints indoor sports will benefit greatly from the modernized Sturrus Sports & Fitness Center. Phase II of the project, which will add indoor practice areas for baseball and softball, will help spring sport athletes train for their season during winter.

Endnotes

1. Aquinas College Catalog, 2010–2011, 4.
2. Aquinas Magazine, Spring 2006, 11.
3. Aquinas College Catalog. 2010–2011, 134.
4. *Aquinas*, Spring 2009, 5.
5. Ibid.

Evolution of the Library

THE LIBRARY ON THE RANSOM STREET CAMPUS was cramped, but students took advantage of the Grand Rapids Public Library's main branch right next door. After the move to the Robinson Road campus in 1945, the former parlor of the manor house became the library for ten years until the construction of the Administration (now Academic) Building. The original plans for AB called for two additional wings to be built, one for a chapel and the other for a library. This plan proved too ambitious to complete in 1955, so the library was "temporarily" housed in one end of the building, with the reference section on the first floor and the circulating library on the second floor. Eventually, the library was consolidated and took up the entire second floor of AB.

As early as 1970, discussion was held about building a freestanding library, but fundraising proved difficult. In 1989, a second attempt was made as part of the Aquinas Grows capital campaign, but the college' s financial crisis cut that drive short. In 1994, President Paul Nelson appointed a Library Committee to study resuming the capital campaign, but, due to more pressing needs, no action was taken until President Harry J. Knopke appointed a new Library Building Committee in 2002. The twelve-member committee, made up of faculty, staff, the provost, and one student representative, visited other libraries, solicited input from the campus, and explored options for adding on to AB, as in the original plan, or of building a totally new building.

After reviewing the campus's "wish list" for the building, one committee member suggested they explore whether the Jarecki Center for Advanced Learning could be adapted into a new library. The building already possessed many of the features requested for the new library, and after compiling information and consulting with Progressive AE, the architects who had built the Jarecki Center, it became clear that the existing building could be adapted and added on to create a new freestanding library while also preserving space for classrooms utilized primarily by the Master of Management Program. It is estimated that the creative adaptation of the old building rather than constructing a totally new one saved the college $6 million.

Thanks to the generosity of local philanthropists Ralph and Grace Hauenstein, ground was broken and construction begun. A professional library moving company was hired to ship the books and materials from the old library to the new one across campus, and in September 2006 the doors of the dramatic new building were opened.

Miss Elizabeth Hightower, right, assistant librarian helps students check out books in the 1940s.

Ralph and Grace Hauenstein whose support made the

Study carrels were crowded in the Woodhouse Library in the Academic Building.

So-called "wet" carrels held video and record machines in the 1980s.

The stacks grew too small for the book holdings in the old library.

» The Hauenstein Library's computers give students access to all the resources of the Internet. The building also allows students to have wireless connections.

The stacks of the Hauenstein Library make an impressive display at night.

Ground is broken for the new Hauenstein Library.

Study group rooms are available on all floors of the Hauenstein Library.

Appendix

Aquinas College Hall of Fame

The Aquinas College Hall of Fame was established in 2002 to recognize individuals whose lifetime contributions to the college and the world at large significantly enhanced the mission of the college. Induction into the Hall of Fame is determined by the Aquinas College Historical Commission, and the formal recognition ceremony takes place each fall. Complete biographies and pictures of the inductees can be found on the Internet at *www.aquinas.edu/heritage/halloffame.*

2011 HALL OF FAME RECIPIENTS

Sister M. Bertrand LaLonde, O.P., Ph.D. †[1]

Scholar of French language, literature, and civilization. Taught at Catholic Junior College and Aquinas College for thirty years. Earned M.A. at University of Notre Dame, additional study in Europe at Universities of Madrid and Friburg, and earned Ph.D. (summa cum laude) at the Sorbonne. Was awarded the Medal of the French Language by the *Academie Francaise* for work on French academician, novelist, and member of the Chamber of Deputies Maurice Barres. Served CJC as directress of studies. Longtime chair of the Aquinas College Departments of French and Spanish. Died in 1977, three months before her one-hundredth birthday after eighty-six years of religious life.

Anthony J. Brink, '43

Graduated in Aquinas College's second graduating class, earned M.F.A. in drama from Catholic University of America and M.A. from Michigan State University. Taught Latin and speech at Aquinas, directed Glee Club from 1948 to 1957. Founded school of music in Florida after leaving Aquinas. Returned to Michigan, earned M.A. in guidance and counseling, Michigan State University. Coordinated Aquinas College's Lansing Extension Program. Devoted member of Alumni Association and active in Catholic affairs in Lansing Diocese where he was program director for Renewal Through Vatican II. Received Alleluia Award for thirty-four years of liturgical service at St. Therese Parish.

Michael Ronan Williams, Ph.D.

Holds five degrees from Regis College, Marquette University, St. Louis University, and University of Wisconsin, Milwaukee. Taught in Milwaukee's inner city during Civil Rights era, co-founded city's first charter school. With wife Mary Alice was active in community service. Joined Aquinas faculty in 1974 to teach education, philosophy, mathematics, and interdisciplinary courses. Chaired the Boards of Eastown Community Association and citywide Council of Neighborhood Associations. With Reverend George Heartwell, developed Aquinas's community leadership major. In 2004 became dean of education until his retirement. Author of two books on education and co-authored *Eastown*.

2010 HALL OF FAME RECIPIENTS

Laurence Burns, '63

Second of eleven siblings to attend Aquinas. On service trip to Bogota, Colombia, Burns and future wife Marion Dougherty became committed to social action. D.O. Kirksville, Missouri College of Osteopathic Medicine. Practiced OB-GYN in Grand Rapids, provided pro bono professional services for impoverished persons and physicals for student athletes. With wife Marion revived Irish Heritage Society of West Michigan.

John O'Connor †

Native of Brooklyn, served in World War II at meteorology school in Grand Rapids, Aleutian Islands, and Trinidad. Accounting instructor at Aquinas in 1960, then two years work with U.S. Agency for International Development. Return to Aquinas, 1964, assistant professor in accounting and part-time controller. Later, full-time controller and vice-president of business and finance. Guided Aquinas through serious financial crises. Retired 1988, died 1999.

Muriel Karp, '48, Ph.D.

Aquinas alumna, biology. M.A. and Ph.D. University of Michigan. Taught University of Michigan and active in caucus for gender equity in salaries and promotions. Worked for NASA Ames Research Center, California. Won Nylen Medal for experiments on correlation between weightlessness and balance and developed computer program for three-dimensional simulation of surgical procedures. After retirement, continued research at University of New Mexico. Inducted into Michigan Women's Hall of Fame for work in medical research and social activism.

2009 HALL OF FAME RECIPIENTS

Bruce Early, Ph.D. †

Aquinas College Music Department, 1971–1999. Began jazz program, organized annual Aquinas College Jazz Festival. Premier influence on local jazz scene for quarter century. Died 1998.

Richard Sedlecky, '51

President of senior class at Aquinas, studied architectural engineering at University of Detroit. Taught as adjunct at Aquinas until 2003. CEO of family construction company in Grand Rapids, structural engineer for URS Greiner, Woodward, Clyde. Supervised international engineering projects. Community service with St. John's Home and Catholic Social Services.

Sister Agnes Thiel, O.P., '62 †

First director of Emeritus College. Formidable advocate for senior citizens for thirty years in Grand Rapids, Kent County, Lansing. Distinguished American Older Volunteer of the Year Award from National Association for the Aging.

2008 PRESIDENT'S AWARD

Anthony J. Foster, M.D., '73

Medical degree Wayne State University, 1977. Physician and surgeon. Private practice in Mecosta County General Hospital in Big Rapids until moving to Grand Rapids in 1987. Attending physician and member of teaching faculty Butterworth and St. Mary's Hospitals, Grand Rapids. Professional appointments include clinical associate professor at Mercy College, Michigan State University Department of Human Services at Butterworth Hospital. General Surgery Division, Michigan Medical, P.C. Medical director for Physician Assistant–Surgical Residency Program, Grand Rapids Medical Education and Research Center. Instrumental support in Aquinas College's Foster Planet Walk and Contemporary Writers Series. First recipient of the President's Award.

2008 HALL OF FAME RECIPIENTS

George LaMountain †

A.B. University of Kansas City, M.A. Catholic University of America. After military service in World War II, came to Aquinas to create Psychology Department. A dominant figure at Aquinas from 1954 to 1982, a "Renaissance Man" and champion of liberal education. Served on Catholic Ecumenical Commission of Grand Rapids Diocese after Vatican II, co-founder of Calvin College–Aquinas College theological discussion group. Described by President Norbert Hruby as a man "of passionate conviction, unquestionable integrity, brilliant and eloquent."

Sister Jean Milhaupt, O.P., Ph.D., '45

An Aquinas College student, faculty member, and archivist since the earliest days of the four-year school. Entered Dominican congregation after 1945 graduation. M.A. Catholic University of America, Ph.D. University of Michigan. Taught literature, grammar, and history of the English language, led study tours to Stratford, Ontario, and Arthurian sites in England. Founded *Sampler*, student literary and art magazine, served on many college committees and taught in Emeritus Program. After 1995 retirement worked as college's archivist. Charter member Aquinas College Historical Commission, collaborator on oral history, dedicated to maintaining Dominican heritage of Aquinas.

Lyle B. Morrison, '52

Community volunteer, United Way, the Development Council of Catholic Secondary Schools. Inducted into Catholic Secondary Schools Hall of Fame. Established Parish Family Center at Immaculate Heart of Mary Parish, served twice as president of Aquinas College Alumni Association. Member of Aquinas College Board of Trustees and Circle Theater Board of Directors. Outstanding Alumni Award 1970, Aquinas Distinguished Service Award 1971. Distinguished Service Awards from Grand Rapids Association of Life Underwriters and the Great West Life Assurance Company, and the Marvin Mullenberg Distinguished Service Award from the State Association of Life Underwriters.

2007 HALL OF FAME RECIPIENTS

Rosemary Fowle Dean, '47, Ph.D.

Aquinas B.A. English. Graduate studies at University of Michigan and Kenyon School of English; Ph.D. University of Chicago. Taught literature and writing at Queens College (City University of New York). Co-author of books on writing: *Beat Not the Poor Desk* and *The Common Sense*. Author of essay collection *Naming the Light*.

Ralph J. Bennett, Ph.D. †

Six earned academic degrees. Professor of accounting and economics at Aquinas College from 1966 to 1996. Initiated Career Action Program (now Continuing Education). Recipient of Sears-Roebuck Foundation Award for Teaching Experience and Campus Leadership. Served with distinction in United States Air Force, the Reserves, and the Michigan National Guard, earning eleven medals and attaining the rank of colonel. Known for tireless energy in the service of students.

Sister Mildred Hawkins, O.P., Ph.D. †

Instrumental in development of Catholic Junior College into Aquinas College. Earned Ph.D. in classical studies from University of Fribourg. Registrar and directress of studies at Catholic Junior College. Brought international faculty to Aquinas College in fields of languages and music. A steadfast advocate for students, the liberal arts, high academic standards, and the primacy of teaching over publication. Died in 1988, aged 101.

2006 HALL OF FAME RECIPIENTS

Joseph '50, and Mary Elizabeth (Beckwith, '50 †) Hansknecht

Met at Aquinas College, married in senior year and earned master's degrees. Joseph taught at Aquinas from 1953 to 1957. Moved to Detroit area where Mary Elizabeth became a leader in Christian Family Movement and Call to Action Coalition. Joseph designed educational program on racism for Detroit archdiocese, was a founding member of Detroit's Urban Alliance, served on Board of Southern Cooperative Development Foundation. Joseph received Bishop Emrich Citation for Outstanding Layman of the Year from the Episcopal Diocese of Michigan and the Human Rights Day Recognition Award from the City of Detroit. Aquinas College Outstanding Alumni Award for both in 1997. Three of their ten children attended Aquinas. In memory of their son Stephen, '83, couple donated money to maintain the Marian Statue and shrine, rededicated in 1989. Mary Elizabeth died in 1996.

Sister Malachi Laithwaite, O.P. †

Librarian, teacher, storyteller, scholar, gardner. Devoted thirty-five years to Catholic Junior College and Aquinas College libraries. Born in Ireland, earned master of library science degree before joining Grand Rapids Dominicans. An authority on children's literature, organizer of Friends of the Aquinas College Library, founding member Story-Spinners League. Awarded honorary doctorate of letters by Aquinas College, 1970. After retirement in 1971, worked with Indian youth in San Juan Pueblo, New Mexico. Died, November 1980 in Grand Rapids.

R. Paul Nelson, President Emeritus

Aquinas College service: associate academic vice president (1969–1973), dean of curriculum (1973–1975), dean of continuing education (1975–1984), dean of student development (1984–1990), interim president and president (1990–1997). Honored by National Association on Career Development for Persons with Disabilities. Known for fostering spirit of community and emphasizing the Dominican heritage of the college. Retired 1997, continued to serve college through courses at Emeritus Program, committee membership.

2005 HALL OF FAME RECIPIENTS

Patrick M. Quinn, '58

Completed Aquinas degree after interruption for military service. Entered food service industry with Nabisco, then Grand Rapids–based D&W Food Centers, eventually became president and CEO of Spartan Stores from 1985 until retirement in 1997. Board service has included Old Kent Bank (now Fifth Third) and numerous Boards related to the food industry. Community service has included United Way, Junior Achievement, American Cancer Society Foundation, Special Olympics, and Racial Justice Institute. Became trustee of Aquinas College in 1987, later first alumnus to serve as chairman of the Board. Granted trustee emeritus status after nine years on Board. Committed service to Catholic Church at parish, diocesan and national levels, including National Advisory Committee to the U.S. Council of Bishops, on the Board of Legatus.

Lewis B. Clingman, Ph.D. †

Served as a historian for U.S. Air Force overseas, joined Aquinas history faculty 1946, served until 1976. Longtime chair of the History Department, leader of the lay faculty. Committed to racial justice and living witness to the Gospel. Charter member of Grand Rapids Human Relations Commission, whose history became the subject of his doctoral dissertation. Consultant for the book *Story of Grand Rapids* (Z. Z. Lydens, ed.), and Michigan Catholic Schools in history. Wife Dorothy, six children, and two grandchildren attended Aquinas, daughter Mary Brigid joined Grand Rapids Dominicans. Lewis died 1976.

Gertrude Horgan †

Joined Aquinas College faculty 1955 after career as vice president Incarnate Word College, San Antonio, and after receiving Gold Medal from Pope Pius XII for service to church. Aquinas career (1955–1979) included service to English Department, and as dean of women. Promoted world literature, black culture, women in literature, and interdisciplinary studies. Established Semester in Ireland Program in 1973. Leader in local Irish Heritage Society, published James Barry's *Tales from the West of Ireland*. Organized service trips to Latin America, served National Council of Catholic Women. Retired in 1979 to Cape Cod, helped establish Wisdom College for retirees. Died 1996.

2004 HALL OF FAME RECIPIENTS

Sister Aquin Gallagher, O.P. †

Graduate degrees in English and journalism, joined faculty of Catholic Junior College, 1933. Advisor for student newspapers at CJC and Aquinas College, awarded medal from Catholic School Press Association. Board of Directors Catholic Renaissance Society of America, helped organize national literary honors society Lambda Iota Tau, received Faith and Service Award of Kappa Gamma Pi, national honor society for women in Catholic colleges. Aquinas College Outstanding Service Award, 1975. Died January 1978.

Norbert Hruby, Ph.D. †

Aquinas College's second president. B.A. University of Chicago, Ph.D. Loyola University. Prior service at University of Chicago and Mundelein College. Initiated Self-Study followed by many innovative programs including Encore, Career Action, Emeritus, Master of Management. Led capital campaign that resulted in Art and Music Center. Initiated Eastown Community Association. Board member and consultant for many educational, religious, and cultural organizations locally and nationally. Honorary doctorates Hope College, Kendall School of Art and Design, and Aquinas College. Retired 1986 and continued writing plays. Died 2010.

C. Arthur Woodhouse †

Financier, executive, Catholic lay leader. Advised all-Dominican Board of Trustees 1940s to 1950s, participated in planning major construction on campus to 1979. Honorary doctorate and Alumni Outstanding Service Award from Aquinas College. Became first lay member of Aquinas Board of Trustees in 1969, remained on Board until 1980. Woodhouse Learning Resources Center dedicated in honor of him and wife Marguerite, 1977. Advisory Board of Grand Rapids Diocese, Resurrection Cemetery, 1959 Diocesan Development Fund. Died 1981, age eighty-four.

2003 HALL OF FAME RECIPIENTS

Marcia (Miller) Clapp, '46 †

Served in numerous capacities from 1960 to 1980, including publicity coordinator, director of publications, and director of public relations/alumni. After Aquinas, public information manager at St. Mary's Hospital in Grand Rapids. Married fellow Aquinas alumnus Charley Clapp, Sr., died 1959. Prior to Aquinas, Marcia worked for *West Michigan Catholic*, freelance writing for the *Grand Rapids Herald*. Aquinas College Outstanding Alumni Award, 1976. Died 1985, age sixty.

Kenneth J. Marin, '47 †

Entered Aquinas College's first class, 1940. Service in World War II as Air Force weather observer in Italy. Completed degree at Aquinas after war. M.A., A.B.D. University of Michigan. Returned to Aquinas, 1953, as faculty member and director of public relations. Founded Aquinas College Credit Union, 1954. President Credit Union National Association, mid-to-late 1960s, elected to Michigan Credit Union Hall of Fame. Aquinas College honorary doctorate, 2001. The six children of Ken and his wife Millie all attended Aquinas College. Ken died 2007.

Sister Aquinas Weber, O.P., '58

Entered Grand Rapids Dominicans 1944, B.A. Aquinas College. Graduate work Catholic

University of America and Marquette University, M.A. University of Michigan (sociology with urban studies focus). Teacher, principal, prioress of Dominican Sisters, Marywood. Service to Aquinas College includes former chair and member College Board of Trustees, director of Emeritus College, vice-president of development, chancellor. Community service includes Board memberships with Greater Grand Rapids Housing Authority, Old Kent Financial Corporation (first woman to serve), Salvation Army, St. John's Home, Gleaners and Hospice of Grand Rapids. Served as director of Eastown Neighborhood Project. Numerous awards including National Jewish Foundation's Tree of Life Award, Notre Dame Award for leadership in Christian ideals, the first Aquinas Reflection Award, the Legacy Award from Greater Grand Rapids Women's History Council.

2002 HALL OF FAME RECIPIENTS

Monsignor Arthur F. Bukowski †

President of Catholic Junior College, then Aquinas College, 1937–1969. Attended St. Joseph Seminary, completed graduate work Catholic University of America and Sulpician Seminary, Washington, D.C. Ordained 1933. Early leader in interracial justice projects and labor relations, chaired Michigan Committee on Civil Rights, served on Michigan Fair Employment Practices Committee. Served on Executive Committee of Association of Independent Colleges and Universities of Michigan (AICUM). Retired from Aquinas, 1969, continued missionary work in Appalachia and Guatemala, taught at St. Joseph Seminary, was director of Society for the Propagation of the Faith, Grand Rapids. Died 1989. Campus pastoral center is named in his honor.

Jerome C. Byrne, '48 †

After Aquinas, attended Harvard Law School, edited *Harvard Law Review*, graduated magna cum laude. Moved to Los Angeles, joined firm of Gibson, Dunn and Crutcher LLP, became partner. Headed Labor and Employment Department. Practiced before U.S. and California Courts of Appeals, U.S. Supreme Court. In 1965, headed University of California team to study student unrest. The influential Byrne Report recommended sweeping changes to U.C. system. Served twelve years on Aquinas Board of Trustees, endowed the prestigious Byrne Scholarship of the Spectrum Scholarship Competition. Died 2001.

Peter M. Wege

Local and international philanthropist. Since 1956, advisor and consultant to Aquinas. Service to college includes thirteen years on Board of Trustees. Major contributor to Aquinas Performing Arts Center. Special benefactor of St. Mary's Mercy Medical Center, the Franciscan Life Center, the Grand Rapids Art Museum. One of the "foremost green thinkers in the design industry," he coined "economicology," encouraging businesses to be environmentally responsible. Founder of Grand Rapids–based Center for Environmental Studies. In 1997, established annual Wege Speaker Series at Aquinas to promote important issues affecting our global community, environment and spirituality.

†Indicates deceased.

Index

About the Author

GARY EBERLE IS A PROFESSOR of English and former chair of the English Department at Aquinas College. Since coming to Aquinas in 1982, he has served as an administrator and faculty member teaching literature and humanities. He founded the Insignis Program for Honors Students in 1985 and was instrumental in initiating the Spectrum Scholarship competition in 1992. A member of the Library Building Committee in 2002, he spearheaded the idea of transforming Jarecki Center into the college's first freestanding library. He has twice been honored with the Student Senate's Outstanding Faculty Member of the Year Award and is the author of seven books, including the novel *Angel Strings* and several nonfiction works, the latest of which is *Dangerous Words: Talking About God in an Age of Fundamentalism*.

Many names, one mission. Aqu

1886–1922

Novitiate Normal School

Teacher training school for Dominican sisters

1922–1927

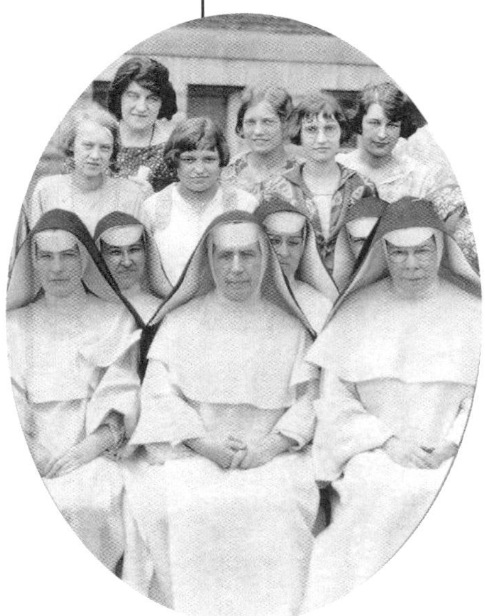

Sacred Heart College

Teacher training for Dominican sisters and lay women

192

Marywood C

Name changed to